DIVINE REVELATION
ACCORDING TO
CHRISTIANITY, JUDAISM, AND ISLAM

DIVINE REVELATION
ACCORDING TO
CHRISTIANITY, JUDAISM, AND ISLAM

A Conversation in Fundamental Theology

Gerald O'Collins, SJ
Marc Rastoin, SJ
Jean-Marc Balhan, SJ

Paulist Press
New York / Mahwah, NJ

The image on the front cover is inspired by the Qur'anic verse: "He brought the two bodies of water together so that they meet one another. Between them lies a barrier that they transgress not. So which of your Lord's boons do you two deny?" (Q 55 The Compassionate: 19-20). This creation by the Egyptian artist Ahmed Moustafa was donated as a sign of gratitude to the Pontifical Gregorian University (Rome, March 30, 1998), where Gerald O'Collins taught, after the exhibition "Where the Two Oceans Meet," which took place on its premises and which was a milestone in the development of Christian-Muslim relations.

Cover design by Sharyn Banks
Book design by Lynn Else

Copyright © 2025 by Gerald O'Collins, Marc Rastoin, and Jean-Marc Balhan

All rights reserved. No part of this publication may be reproduced, stored in a retrieval system, or transmitted in any form or by any means, electronic, mechanical, photocopying, recording, scanning, or otherwise, without either the prior written permission of the Publisher, or authorization through payment of the appropriate per-copy fee to the Copyright Clearance Center, Inc., www.copyright.com. Requests to the Publisher for permission should be addressed to the Permissions Department, Paulist Press, permissions@paulistpress.com.

Library of Congress Cataloging-in-Publication Data
Names: O'Collins, Gerald, author. | Rastoin, Marc, 1967– author. | Balhan, Jean-Marc, author.
Title: Divine revelation according to Christianity, Judaism, and Islam: a conversation in fundamental theology / Gerald O'Collins, SJ, Marc Rastoin, SJ, and Jean Marc Balhan, SJ.
Description: Paperback. | New York: Paulist Press, [2025] | Includes index. | Summary: "A conversation among experts in Christian, Jewish, and Muslim theology on the similarities and differences in fundamental theology—especially in the area of divine revelation—among the three Abrahamic religions"—Provided by publisher.
Identifiers: LCCN 2024051585 (print) | LCCN 2024051586 (ebook) | ISBN 9780809157280 (paperback) | ISBN 9780809188963 (ebook)
Subjects: LCSH: Revelation—Comparative studies. | Abrahamic religions.
Classification: LCC BL475.5 .O34 2025 (print) | LCC BL475.5 (ebook) | DDC 212/.6—dc23/eng/20250113
LC record available at https://lccn.loc.gov/2024051585
LC ebook record available at https://lccn.loc.gov/2024051586

ISBN 978-0-8091-5728-0 (paperback)
ISBN 978-0-8091-8896-3 (ebook)

Published by Paulist Press
997 Macarthur Boulevard
Mahwah, NJ 07430
www.paulistpress.com

Printed and bound in the
United States of America

To Paolo Dall'Oglio, SJ (b. 1954, kidnapped in Syria, presumed killed in 2013). He revived the Deir Mar Musa community (80 miles north of Damascus), where he worked for decades in promoting Muslim-Christian dialogue.

CONTENTS

Preface ix
   Gerald O'Collins

Abbreviations xiii

1. Contacts with Judaism and Islam in
   My Fundamental Theology 1
      Gerald O'Collins

   Perspective from Judaism 22
      Marc Rastoin

   Perspective from Islam 25
      Jean-Marc Balhan

2. "So Near and Yet So Far": How Do Jews Do Theology? 29
      Marc Rastoin

   Perspective from Christianity 43
      Gerald O'Collins

   Perspective from Islam 47
      Jean-Marc Balhan

3. The Modalities of Revelation in Islam 51
      Jean-Marc Balhan

   Perspective from Christianity 89
      Gerald O'Collins

CONTENTS

Perspective from Judaism 93
    Marc Rastoin

Epilogue 97
    Gerald O'Collins

Notes 101

Index 123

Contributors 127

PREFACE

> The notion of revelation in Judaism and Islam has a paramount role in any [Christian] comparative understanding of revelation.
>
> Balázs Mezei, *The Oxford Handbook of Divine Revelation*, xxiv

SOME READERS MIGHT react negatively to a book on divine self-revelation (and related questions in fundamental theology) as proposed by Christianity, Judaism, and Islam being produced by three Jesuits. Surely a Jewish scholar should have contributed the proposal of Judaism? Why did a Muslim scholar not offer the Islamic stance of faith? The Jewish professor I had in mind died. I turned to another Jewish scholar whom I knew; he was overwhelmed by a battery of engagements.

Marc Rastoin's studies on the identity of Paul the Apostle, along with his teaching in Paris and Rome, have put him in fruitful contact with Jewish religious thought. Jean-Marc Balhan has lived for years in Turkey and engaged in dialogue with Muslim intellectuals. Sympathetic "outsiders" can understand the beliefs and commitments of those who embrace other faiths and cultural agenda. The French Count Alexis de Tocqueville (1805–59), while an outsider to the American democratic experiment, understood and interpreted its values and risks in a remarkable fashion.

DIVINE REVELATION ACCORDING TO CHRISTIANITY, JUDAISM, AND ISLAM

As an Italian proverb states, "We never forget our first love" (*il primo amore non si scorda mai*). Foundational or fundamental theology and its major topics (the divine self-revelation that elicits faith, the tradition that hands on the experience of revelation, and the biblical inspiration that produces texts (to recall, interpret, and apply episodes of revelation) sparked my first love as a researcher, teacher, and writer. This branch of theology, which can substantially coincide with "philosophical theology," has remained the love of a lifetime.

After a PhD at the University of Cambridge on some modern views of revelation (1968), I published *Theology and Revelation* (Cork: Mercier Press, 1968), *Foundations of Theology* (Chicago: Loyola University Press, 1971), *Fundamental Theology* (New York: Paulist Press, 1981), *Problems and Perspectives of Fundamental Theology* (coedited with René Latourelle, New York: Paulist Press, 1982), *Retrieving Fundamental Theology* (Mahwah, NJ: Paulist Press, 1993), *Rethinking Fundamental Theology* (Oxford: Oxford University Press, 2011), and other books, chapters in books, and articles on particular aspects of fundamental theology, which include the resurrection of the crucified Jesus—right down to *Revelation* (Oxford: Oxford University Press, 2016), *Inspiration* (Oxford: Oxford University Press, 2018), and *Tradition* (Oxford: Oxford University Press, 2018).

Fundamental theology takes up the themes of divine revelation, human faith, tradition, and biblical inspiration, while responding to changes in cultural, ecclesial, economic, and political realities. Its growth has also come through respecting and learn from Jewish and Islamic insights into revelation, tradition, and the inspired Scriptures.

In the Middle Ages, exchanges flourished among Christian thinkers and their Jewish (think Avicebron and Maimonides) and Muslim (think Averroes and Avicenna) counterparts. Similar exchanges continue. Marc Rastoin and Jean-Marc Balhan, experts in Judaism and Islam, respectively, have joined me in reflecting on foundational themes of Jewish and Islamic theology that converge with or differ from their counterparts in Christian fundamental theology. Their expertise retrieves a golden past and develops for it a comparative approach.

PREFACE

My thanks also go out to Rev. Professor Russell Goulbourne, former Dean of the Faculty of Arts at the University of Melbourne and a noted French scholar. He translated into English the chapter by Marc Rastoin. The other texts by Rastoin and Balhan, also written in French, were translated by me into English.

Jewish and Muslim scholars do not regularly use the term *fundamental theology*, but their accounts of revelation, faith, tradition, and Scripture throw light on these themes which constitute the core of Christian fundamental theology. Similarities and contrasts enrich our personal insights. As Mezei writes in *The Oxford Handbook of Divine Revelation*, "the notion of revelation in Judaism and Islam has a paramount role in any [Christian] comparative understanding of revelation" (xxiv). This could mean studying Emmanuel Lévinas's Talmudic theology. Two chapters of his *Beyond the Verse: Talmudic Readings and Lectures* (Bloomington: Indiana University Press, 1994) examine "Revelation in the Jewish Tradition" and "On the Jewish Reading of Scriptures."

As regards Judaism and Islam, the fourth edition of *The Oxford Dictionary of the Christian Church* (Oxford: Oxford University Press, 2022) supplies entries such as "Halakhah," "Islam, Christian Engagement with," "Judaism," and "Judaism, Christian Writers on," along with entries on such thinkers as Averroes, Avicenna, Martin Buber, Abraham Heschel, Lévinas, Philo of Alexandria, Maimonides, and Ludwig Wittgenstein.

I regularly follow with gratitude the New Revised Standard Version (NRSV). Very occasionally I adopt my own translation.

My thanks go out to Paul Avis, Michael Barnes, David Braithwaite, Julian Butler, Brendan Byrne, Manfred Cain, Charlotte Clements, Sarah Coakley, Stephen Curtin, Isaac Demase, Donna Crilly, Lisa Gerber, Justin Glyn, and Ormond Rush. In various ways they helped create this book.

In the terminology of "the Old Testament," rather than the "Tanakh" or Hebrew Bible as in the Jewish tradition, "old" is understood as "good" and does not imply "supersessionism," the view that the New Testament has rendered obsolete the Old Testament.

DIVINE REVELATION ACCORDING TO
CHRISTIANITY, JUDAISM, AND ISLAM

I dedicate this book to the inspiring memory of a fellow Jesuit, Paolo Dall'Oglio (b. 1954, kidnapped in Syria, and presumed killed in 2013). A former student of mine at the Gregorian University (Rome), he revived the Deir Mar Musa community (eighty miles north of Damascus), where he worked for decades in promoting Muslim-Christian dialogue.

Gerald O'Collins, SJ

ABBREVIATIONS

EI	Peter Bearman et al., eds., *Encylopedia of Islam*, 12 vols., 2nd ed. (Leiden: Brill, 1960–2009).
EQ	J. D. MacAuliffe, ed., *Encyclopedia of the Qur'an*, 5 vols. (Leiden: Brill, 2001–2006).
ODCC	Andrew Louth, ed., *The Oxford Dictionary of the Christian Church*, 4th ed. (Oxford: Oxford University Press, 2022).
OHDivRev	Balázs M. Mezei, Francesca Aran Murphy, and Kenneth Oakes, eds., *The Oxford Handbook of Divine Revelation* (Oxford: Oxford University Press, 2021).
Q	M. A. S. Abdel Haleem, *The Qur'an* (Oxford: Oxford University Press, 2005).

1
CONTACTS WITH JUDAISM AND ISLAM IN MY FUNDAMENTAL THEOLOGY

Gerald O'Collins, SJ

AFTER A LIFETIME OF expounding the themes of Christian fundamental theology, I want to pin down contacts with Jewish and Muslim religious culture that I experienced over the years. How have those contacts affected, directly or indirectly, my theology?

Personal Contacts

Sir Isaac Isaacs, the first native-born governor general of the Commonwealth of Australia (1931–36) and the first Jew to serve in that office, had been a colleague of my maternal grandfather in legal and political life. That contact kept our home free from anti-Semitism. So, too, did Sir John Monash (1865–1931), an outstanding general under whom my father served in France during the First World War.

My family knew quite well the second Jewish governor general (also native-born), Sir Zelman Cowen, a dean of the law school at the University of Melbourne, where my father, I myself, four of my five siblings, and many other relatives studied. After years as governor general (1977–82), Zelman became provost of Oriel College, Oxford (1982–90). Before returning to Australia, he visited St. John Paul II in Rome and pressed the case for the pope to canonize, or at least beatify, a famous fellow of Oriel, John Henry Newman, in whose memory Oriel had prepared a small shrine. In effect, the pope told Zelman that "Newman had failed his practicals." At that point, no miracles had been accepted to support Newman's rise to the altar. However, before he died in 2011, Zelman had the satisfaction of learning that a miracle had been certified and John Henry Newman declared Blessed in 2010.

Between finishing my PhD at Cambridge University and starting full-time at the Gregorian University, I taught as a visiting professor at Weston College (Boston Theological Institute) for five semesters from 1968 to 1972. I came to know Harry Wolfson, a Harvard University Jewish scholar and world expert on Philo of Alexandria (ca. 25 BCE–ca. 50 CE), arguably the greatest Jewish theologian of all time.[1] Unfortunately, I did little to seize the chance of doing some informal study of Philo with Wolfson.

During doctoral studies at Cambridge University (1965–68), I might have studied Islam with Arthur Arberry. An outstanding Islamic scholar, he was a fellow of Pembroke College, the very college where I was a research fellow. His translation of the Qur'an was widely used, and he had proved himself an outstanding interpreter of Sufi mysticism. A few years later, teaching summer programs at the University of Notre Dame offered a similar possibility to profit from the Islamic learning of David Burrell.[2] But I failed to take advantage of this golden opportunity.

Later in Rome, I did learn about Islam—not least from Daniel Madigan, SJ, a colleague at the Gregorian University from 2000 to 2006. He created and headed the Gregorian Centre for Interreligious Studies until his departure in 2007 for Georgetown University, Washington, DC. I profited from contacts with visiting Muslims. In May 1989, for instance, a group of Turkish Muslims from the

CONTACTS WITH JUDAISM AND ISLAM IN MY FUNDAMENTAL THEOLOGY

University of Ankara shared discussions at the Gregorian University, which entered into a covenant of collaboration with their university. Through April 1998, the Gregorian hosted an exhibition, *Where Two Oceans Meet*, works created by a leading Muslim artist from Egypt, Ahmed Moustafa. To thank the Gregorian for hosting the exhibition, he gave us a painting of *The Two Seas*, easily the most valuable work of art on our campus. Under Madigan's leadership, the Centre for Interreligious Studies, now active alongside the Cardinal Bea Centre for Judaic Studies, flourished and brought valuable contacts with Muslim teachers and students.

Islamic theology entered a doctoral thesis written in Italian under my direction by a Polish priest, Aleksander Mazur, on *L'insegnamento di Giovanni Paolo II sulle altre religioni* (The teaching of John Paul II on other religions).[3] Mazur's extensive bibliography set itself to include every piece of papal teaching on the topic from 1978 to 2000.[4] He informed me about the papal teaching on Islam. The outstanding document remains the 1985 address to young Muslims in Morocco, a landmark in the history of Catholic relations with Islam. In *Pope John Paul II: A Reader*, which I coedited, the Morocco address, cited in its entirely, forms the largest part (148–58) in the section on interreligious dialogue (146–67).[5]

With Steve Davis and Dan Kendall, SJ, I organized meetings in New York on the Resurrection of Christ (1996), Trinity (1998), Incarnation (2000), and Redemption (2003), with the proceedings published in four books by Oxford University Press. On each occasion a Jewish scholar, the late Alan Segal, was part of the team; he contributed a chapter to the first volume (on resurrection). Another Jewish professor, Peter Ochs of the University of Virginia, attended the fourth meeting and contributed his chapter to the volume on redemption. I hoped that the presence of Jewish scholars would keep the rest of us, all Christians and coming from several denominations, tied to our ancient, religious roots.

Elder brothers and sisters of Christians, Jews constituted the chosen people long before any disciples embraced faith in Jesus. The old Roman Canon, for many centuries the only eucharistic prayer used in the Latin rite, evoked the memory of Abraham, "our father in faith." Jews have been senior members in a family of faith that has accepted the divine self-revelation in a history that stretches back to Abraham and Sarah, our parents in faith.

After leaving the Gregorian University in 2006 and before returning to Australia in 2009, I enjoyed a research chair at St. Mary's College (now St. Mary's University), Twickenham. Michael Hayes, the head of the School of Theology, Philosophy, and History, organized with me a conference on the legacy of Pope John Paul II. The book that resulted contained a chapter on the pope and Catholic-Jewish dialogue, along with two notable chapters by Christian Troll, SJ, on, respectively, relations with Islam and the Muslim prophetic view of Muhammad.[6]

After returning to Melbourne, I published *The Second Vatican Council on Other Religions*,[7] which, apropos of the relevant sections of Vatican II's teaching, examined Islam but had little to say about Judaism. As a Christian I shrink from treating the Jewish faith among "the other religions." In any case I had already presented pertinent Old Testament beliefs and practices in *Salvation for All: God's Other Peoples*.[8]

Philosophy

Let me recall areas of Christian fundamental theology in which Jewish sources enrich our understanding: philosophy, doctrine of God, and the human situation that God addresses.

First, philosophy: in the advice offered to young theologians in my *Rethinking Fundamental Theology* is the invitation to "be philosophical."[9] I might have added, "and make sure you read modern Jewish philosophers like Ernst Bloch, Martin Buber, Emmanuel Levinas, Edith Stein, Simone Weil, and Ludwig Wittgenstein." Three Jewish grandparents, as well as other influences, gave Wittgenstein a deep Jewish heritage. Before leaving the University of Cambridge after my PhD in 1968, I visited his tomb in a local cemetery and felt strengthened in a conviction that might have come from him—that theology means watching our language in the presence of God. Wittgenstein had been the dominant philosopher during my years at the University of Melbourne (1949, 1955–58). Students learned his advice to prefer asking about the use of words, not their meaning.

I featured Wittgenstein in the unfinished postscript to my *Easter Faith: Believing in the Risen Jesus*. Such faith responds to the good news of the risen Christ "believingly—i.e. lovingly. It is love that believes the Resurrection." Wittgenstein recalled a bleak alternative: "If he [Christ] did not rise from the dead, then he decomposed in the grave like any other man. *He is dead and decomposed.* In that case he is a teacher like any other and can no longer *help*; and once more we are orphaned and alone."[10]

The dialogical I–Thou philosophy of Buber sent me on a pilgrimage to Heppenheim, a charming town near the banks of the Rhine. Nightingales sing through the darkness, and Buber enjoyed a home there for many years (1916–38).

At the University of Tübingen, I visited Ernst Bloch (1885–1977) on the banks of the Neckar River. A thatch of white hair, the thick-lensed glasses, and his lined face gave him the look of a latter-day prophet. He feared that theologians were taming his utopian, neo-Marxist views, "spreading hotel sauce over everything," as he put it. At the time he was writing *Atheismus und Christentum*.[11] I expressed regret that his works had not been translated into English and subsequently wrote an article about Bloch's influence on contemporary theologians (highlighting Jürgen Moltmann's theology of hope), "The Principle and Theology of Hope."[12]

In the winter of 1967–68, Justus George Lawler invited me to translate Bloch's *Das Prinzip Hoffnung* for Herder and Herder. I enthusiastically supported the project, declined it myself (given the sheer size of Bloch's great work), and offered to write a book on the theology of hope. The result was *Man [!] and His New Hopes*, which, endorsed by Moltmann, appeared the following year.[13] A visiting TV group from West Germany joined the Harvard theologian Harvey Cox in giving this book a gala launch in Cambridge, Massachusetts.

God: Challenges to and Attributes of

Bloch's Jewish philosophy of hope provided language for understanding God (as the "coming" or Advent God of Rev 1:8) and for unfolding the future-oriented human condition reflected in Vatican II's *Gaudium et Spes* (Joy and Hope), the Pastoral Constitution on the Church that closed the Council in December 1965.

The Hebrew Scriptures, not least the second half of Isaiah (Isa 40—66) and the apocalyptic Book of Daniel, encouraged Gerhard von Rad, professor at the University of Heidelberg, to summarize the history of a community's "ever increasing expectations" (read "human hopes sparked by divine promises").[14] Moltmann's lectures at Tübingen and publications had put at center stage Isaiah's oracle, "do not remember the former things, or consider the things of old. I am about to do a new thing" (Isa 43:18–19). This promise returns in Revelation 21:5: "See, I am making all things new."

As Mezei observes in *The Oxford Handbook of Divine Revelation*, "talking *about* God is intrinsically about talking *to* God, and talking to God is always made possible and actual by God talking to us."[15] Mezei echoes a traditional account of revelation as *locutio Dei* (the speaking/talking of God). Here one needs to reflect on the existence and attributes of God who talks to us and who announces the renewal of creation in the coming of "the new heavens and the new earth" (Rev 21:1–8).

Christian, Jewish, and Muslim believers accept a personal God who has entered into a self-revealing relationship with them and with the communities to which they belong. Many believers would add that there are good reasons for accepting that God exists and cares about them deeply. Many are also keenly aware of challenges to their faith. Where was God in Auschwitz? Where was God in the tsunami of Christmas 2004? Has modern science made belief in God obsolete?

CONTACTS WITH JUDAISM AND ISLAM IN MY FUNDAMENTAL THEOLOGY

Is the concept of an all-powerful, all-good, and all-knowing God incoherent in itself? Or worse, are faith in God and religious practice not only irrational, but also socially and morally destructive?[16]

New atheists such as Richard Dawkins and Christopher Hitchens deserve thanks for bringing God questions into popular debate. But Hitchens turned preposterous with his claim that "religion poisons everything."[17] Dawkins has tried to explain—or should we say explain away?—his objections to Islam. In facing challenges to faith in God, I prefer debate with such classical opponents as the Scottish philosopher David Hume and the twentieth-century Jew, Sigmund Freud.

Freud argued that human reason and experience could not be reconciled with the doctrines of religious faith: "Religious doctrines will have to be discarded. You know why: in the long run nothing can withstand reason and experience, and the contradiction which religion offers to both is all too palpable."[18] Elsewhere,[19] I debated Freud's rejection of what he called "the grandiose" commandment: "you shall love your neighbor as yourself" (Mark 12:31), cited by Jesus from Leviticus 19:18.[20] For Freud this was an impossible demand that caused crippling guilt.

In presenting the existence and attributes of our personal God, I have drawn from the Old Testament theologies of such scholars as Gerhard von Rad and directly from the New Oxford Annotated Bible.[21] It has notable Jewish scholars among its associate editors and many contributors (such as Marc Z. Brettler, Amy-Jill Levine, and Bernard M. Levinson).

The divine self-revelation in the history of Israel produced a gradual purification in the people's understanding of the God of Abraham, Isaac, and Jacob. A divine pedagogy led them to the insights and language of Second Isaiah, which, through their place in Georg Friedrich Handel's *Messiah*, have permanently affected the imagination and faith of millions of Christians.[22] Other passages of Isaiah became a deep reservoir from which believers drew fresh understanding of God. The acclamation "Holy, holy, holy" (Isa 6:3),

DIVINE REVELATION ACCORDING TO CHRISTIANITY, JUDAISM, AND ISLAM

which acknowledged the sacred otherness of the enthroned Lord, would be repeated in the Book of Revelation (Rev 4:8) and give rise to the Jewish *Kedusha*, the Roman Christian *Sanctus*, and the *Trisagion* in the Eastern liturgy. The full Hebrew Bible witnesses to the essential attributes of God, disclosed as eternal, totally spiritual, truly and fully personal, utterly holy, omnipotent, and possessed of unlimited power, perfect goodness, and unlimited knowledge. Such a divine Being must command unconditional admiration, praise, and worship on the part of human beings.

Except for some passages in Wisdom literature, the Old Testament witness to God comes less in the second-order language of theological statements than in the first-order language of religious speech. This is the language attributed to the Lord by Second Isaiah: "Can a woman forget her nursing child, or show no compassion for the child of her womb? Even these may forget, yet I will not forget you. See, I have inscribed you on the palms of my hands" (Isa 49:15–16).

Rudolf Otto's successful term for the divine holiness, *mysterium tremendum et fascinans* (the awesome and fascinating mystery),[23] fits the story of Moses drawn to see the mysterious bush that was burning but not being consumed. But Moses must remove the sandals from his feet, for he was standing on holy ground. Moses "hid his face, for he was afraid to look at God" (Exod 3:1–6).

One could also speak of the Jewish Scriptures presenting God as both mysteriously other and intimately close. God displays a coincidence of divine transcendence and immanence. A deceased friend of mine, Peter Steele, spoke of a "strangeness beyond description" and a "nearness beyond denying." God is not only the numinous Stranger beyond strangeness but also the very air we breathe and a nearness beyond denying.

This is a nearness illustrated by the Psalms, which pour out to God feelings of sorrow, lamentation, fear, praise, and happiness, as well as witnessing to the astonishing mystery of God. The New Testament cites, or at least echoes, 129 psalms out of the 150 that constitute the Psalter. Christians received them as authoritative and followed Paul and the Gospels in using them to interpret the revelation conveyed through the missions of the Son and the Holy Spirit. History testifies repeatedly to the inspiring impact of the psalms on the communal and individual life of Christians, Jews, and others.[24]

Two extraordinary characteristics of the Jewish psalms frequently escape attention. First, these poetic prayers record ways in which human beings have received and interpreted *the divine revelation* communicated through history and creation. The psalms highlight the loving faithfulness of God whom the Israelites experienced in events of history and the works of creation. Second, the book of Jewish prayer, the Psalter, became *the Christian book of prayer*. The divine office, Christian liturgy, and personal prayer live through the psalms, supplemented by a few New Testament prayers (above all, the Lord's Prayer, the *Benedictus*, and the *Magnificat*). As much as and even more than other prayers, the psalms embody central images of God and of human beings who take these images into their prayer life.

The Human Beings Receive Revelation in Faith

Having recalled themes for a doctrine of God mindful of Judaism, we move to those who in faith (and with hope and love) accept divine revelation. What account might we give of the human condition?

We could speak of *homo dolens*, human beings who suffer through what they have lost and continue to lose, as well as through what they fear about the present and the future. Loss, sometimes terrible loss, and fear characterize the lives of men and women everywhere. In a poem written in the Second World War, "*Ecce homo*," David Gascoyne (1916–2001) pictured the awful story of human pain. By quoting Blaise Pascal's *Pensée* 552, Gascoyne linked all suffering to the suffering of Christ: "He is in agony till the world's end, / And we must never sleep during that time!"[25] Among the victims

DIVINE REVELATION according to
CHRISTIANITY, JUDAISM, and ISLAM

"in agony," the poet named Jews. His verbal picture drove home the message of a 1938 painting by the Jewish artist Marc Chagall (1887–1985), *White Crucifixion*.

Jesus Christ drew near to Jews and all human beings. His body on the cross expressed his presence to those who experience pain anywhere and at any time. The death between two criminals of God's Suffering Servant (Isa 52:13—53:12) symbolized forever Christ's solidarity with those who suffer and die. We might say: *ubi dolor ibi Christus* (wherever there is suffering, there is Christ). A *homo dolens* version of the human condition writes large what the Jewish philosopher and Nobel Laureate Elie Wiesel (1928–2016) recalled from the horrors he experienced at the Auschwitz and Buchenwald camps and recalled in *Night*.[26]

Another survivor from Auschwitz and the founder of logotherapy, the Jewish psychiatrist Viktor Frankl (1905–97) understood the struggle to find meaning as the principal driving force in human beings. As ceaseless questioners (*homo interrogans*), children exemplify the quest for meaning and truth that they are born with. Sooner or later, we ask ourselves: where do we come from? Who are we? What does our existence mean—in its sinful failures, apparent successes, and future destiny? Is there a supreme Being in whose presence we play out our lives? Do we meet that Being beyond death?[27]

Artists and writers have often expressed the questing and questioning spirit of *homo interrogans*. Shortly before his death in Tahiti, the Postimpressionist painter Paul Gauguin (1848–1903) wrote out three questions on a large triptych he had completed: "Where do we come from? What are we? Where are we going?" Classic writers, such as Dante Alighieri (1265–1321), Leo Tolstoy (1828–1910), and Fyodor Dostoyevsky (1821–81), have constantly raised these eternal questions. A *homo interrogans* vision of humanity aligns itself with a tradition that goes back to the radical questions of Paul (Rom 7:13–25), the Psalms (above all, Ps 22, the prayer of a person "abandoned" by God), and Job 38:1—42:6—a tradition that understands revelation as answers correlating with these questions about meaning and pain.

The Personal Self-Revelation of God

At a time that often neglects the biblical witness to the divine self-revelation through the *acta Dei* (the activity of God) and the *locutio Dei* (discourse of God), it has been a relief to read the 720-page *Oxford Handbook of Divine Revelation*.[28] This work, a collaboration of forty-two contributors, includes chapters on revelation in the Jewish tradition and revelation in Islam.[29] For good measure, the handbook contains chapters on revelation in Hindu and Buddhist traditions, revelation according to Confucianism, and revelation in West and Central African faiths.

Revelation, wherever it occurs, is primarily a personal, transforming I–Thou (see Martin Buber or, better, We–You) encounter with God, and secondarily the disclosure of hitherto unknown truths about God and human beings. For Christians, it is supremely the divine self-communication in the person of Jesus and through the Holy Spirit, a self-manifestation of the ultimate *Truth* (uppercase and singular) rather than God making known a set of *truths* (lowercase and plural) otherwise inaccessible to human beings.

Up to the twentieth century, many people held a propositional view of revelation, or revelation as new and precious information formerly inaccessible but now freely made available by God and to be accepted on divine authority. The impact of notable theologians,[30] the teaching of Vatican II in its 1965 Dogmatic Constitution on Divine Revelation, *Dei Verbum* (the Word of God), and other influences—not least the contribution of biblical (both Old and New Testament) and liturgical studies and personalist philosophies—established the primary model of revelation as God's personal self-disclosure. The propositional view remained but moved into second place. Those who know God through experiencing revelation and embracing new faith commitments, such as Abraham, Moses, Isaiah, Peter the apostle, Mary Magdalene, and Paul of Tarsus, can then speak about God and communicate new and previously inaccessible information. Knowledge of God leads to knowledge about God.

Means, Mediators, and Mystery of Revelation

Revelation may take place through special, dramatic *means*, such as Moses's encounter at the burning bush, the return from the Babylonian exile, the miracles performed by Jesus, and his resurrection from the dead. The *mediators* of revelation may also be special persons—for example, the Jewish prophets, the twelve apostles, Paul, and Jesus himself. But divine revelation can also be communicated through such ordinary realities as daily prayer, the birth of a child, common worship, or experiences of suffering. Those who mediate revelation can be ordinary human beings, not necessarily kind and self-giving persons, but even vicious persons whose cruel deeds unwittingly disclose the loving presence of God and God's Suffering Servant. The case of David committing adultery and murder shows how such grave sins can prove the occasion for divine revelation to be communicated—a revelation about David's state before God and future destiny (2 Sam 11—12). When we think of the means and mediators of divine self-revelation, the whole Bible and not least the Jewish Scriptures point to endless possibilities.

The Jewish and Christian Scriptures record and interpret much that bears directly on God's self-revelation. We live in the presence of Absolute Mystery and not merely Mystery.[31] Revelation enhances rather than removes the utter mysteriousness of God. The more one knows God, the more mysterious God becomes.

"The LORD used to speak to Moses *face to face*, as one speaks to a friend" (Exod 33:11; see Num 12:78; Deut 24:10). Yet, after God revealed the Ten Commandments, "the people stood at a distance, while Moses drew near to *the thick darkness* where God was" (Exod 20:21). When God wrote again the Ten Commandments, Moses went up Mount Sinai: "The LORD descended *in the cloud* and stood with him there and proclaimed the name, 'The LORD,'" and *disclosed himself* as "the LORD, the LORD, a God merciful and gracious, slow to anger, and abounding in steadfast love and faithfulness" (Exod 34:4–6).

First Kings provides another example of God understood to be present and revealed in a cloud and even in "thick darkness," When the priests brought the ark of the covenant into Solomon's temple, "a cloud filled the house of the LORD, so that the priests could not stand to minister because of the cloud. Then Solomon said: 'The LORD has said that he would dwell in *thick darkness*'" (8:10–12). A sense of God being present and revealed in thick darkness prompted Gregory of Nyssa to reflect on a revelation that enhances and does not take away the mysterious divine hiddenness.[32]

Jesus the Fullness of Revelation

A study of the teaching and activity of Jesus belongs squarely to the heart of Christian fundamental theology. A bibliography could include not only works by Kenneth E. Bailey, Richard Bauckham, James Dunn, Paul R. Eddy and Gregory A. Boyd, Martin Hengel, Craig S. Keener, Gerhard Lohfink, John P. Meier, and David Wenham,[33] but also commentaries on Mark (e.g., by Joel Marcus), Matthew (e.g., by Ulrich Luz), and Luke (e.g., by François Bovon).[34] Attention should also be paid to such Jewish scholars who have taught and written on the Gospels as Amy-Jill Levine (b. 1956) and Jacob Neusner (1932–2016). They and others, such as Géza Vermes (1924–2013), have partly succeeded in convincing the Christian public that ignoring the Jewishness of Jesus threatens any balanced interpretation of him. Denying that Jesus was a Jew belongs to the lethal anti-Semitism that inspired the Holocaust and brought the murder of Vermes's own parents.

When acknowledging the divine self-revelation in Christ to be complete, we should hear the warnings of Jacques Dupuis about not slipping into the mistake of calling it definitive. To be full, complete, and perfect is one thing, but to be definitive goes further. It would mean that this revelation has proved unconditionally full, totally complete, and simply conclusive, so that all God's revelation is over and done with.³⁵ "Definitive" is incompatible with the gap between the historical revelation in Jesus Christ and the final, glorious revelation at the *eschaton* (e.g., Titus 2:13 and 1 Tim 6:14).

The Resurrection of Jesus

I have entered debate with resurrection deniers, since measured apologetics in this field belong to Christian fundamental theology. My background theory presupposed that Easter faith is reasonable if it is not illogical, proves compatible with well-established beliefs, and has plausible foundations in enriching human experience.³⁶

Debate about the resurrection involved two Holocaust survivors, Paul Jakob Winter (1904–69) and Géza Vermès, who prepared a revised edition of Winter's book.³⁷ Winter expressed the view that "resurrection" affected the disciples of Jesus, but not Jesus himself. The "something" that happened after his death and burial was only a change in them, not a new, transformed life for Jesus.

> Crucified, dead and buried, he yet rose in the hearts of his disciples who had loved him and felt that he was near. Tried by the world, condemned by authority, buried by the Churches that profess his name, he is rising again, today and tomorrow in the hearts of men who love him and feel: he is near.³⁸

Such change-of-heart theory must deny or distort the meaning of what the first Christians (e.g., Paul in 1 Cor 15:3–5) and other New Testament authors (e.g., the four evangelists) say again and again. Although appearing to claim some new fact about Jesus (his personal resurrection to glorious life), they allegedly used a deceptive form of discourse and talked only about a powerful, seminal idea that now possessed their minds and hearts.

Vermès in *Jesus the Jew*³⁹ proposed the same thesis, which

"under-interprets" the Christian witness to the resurrection. Paul and further New Testament authors, although seeming to claim the personal resurrection of Jesus, were talking only about a fresh faith and love that now filled their hearts. The title of the epilogue to Vermès's book enunciates this thesis: "Resurrection [Merely] in the Hearts of Men." The thesis misrepresents what the New Testament witnesses proclaim.

Other Jews, however, have recognized the scope of that proclamation and accepted its truth without seeking to become Christian believers. Probably the most famous writer among such Jews has been the rabbi Pinchas Lapide.[40] While acknowledging that the crucified Jesus had been raised from the dead, he claimed that the resurrection established Jesus as the Savior of the Gentiles but not as the Messiah of the Jews.

Sometimes Jewish authors nominate conditions for acknowledging Jesus risen from the dead. Rabbi Dan Cohn-Sherbok sets out such a scenario:

> If Jesus appeared surrounded by hosts of angels trailing clouds of glory and announcing his Messiahship for all to see, this would certainly be compelling. But it would have to take place in the public domain. Such an event would have to be witnessed by multitudes, photographed, recorded on video cameras, shown on television, and announced in newspapers and magazines worldwide. Jesus' appearance would have to be a global event, televised on CNN and other forms of the world's media. Further, if as a consequence of his arrival, all the prophecies recorded in the scriptures were fulfilled, the ingathering of the exiles, the rebuilding of the Temple, the resurrection of all those who have died, the advent of the Days of the Messiah, final judgement—I would without doubt embrace the Christian message and become a follower of the risen Christ.[41]

Such compelling evidence belongs, however, to Jesus's second coming at the end-time rather than to the era between Jesus and the *eschaton* in which we now live. Moreover, overwhelming reasons would rule out the possibility of freely committing oneself to Jesus and becoming his follower. Believing in a person, we can point to good reasons for doing so but not to utterly coercive reasons. There is evidence, but faith goes beyond the evidence in a loving commitment.

Faith in Jesus

The Gospel of John offers a narrative theology of human faith initiated by Christ. In his encounters with individuals (and groups of people), Jesus presents himself as the Revealer and the Revelation of God and invites the response of faith.

Sometimes the individuals who meet Jesus are given names, such as Andrew (1:35–42), Nicodemus (3:1–15), Martha (11:17–27), Mary Magdalene (20:1–18), and Peter (21:15–19). Sometimes they are simply called a Samaritan woman (4:1–42), a royal official (4:43–54), a man who has been disabled for thirty-eight years (5:1–18), a woman taken in adultery (7:53—8:11),[42] and a man born blind (9:1–41). All but one of these persons (the Samaritan woman) are Jews. We can spot recurrent needs of human beings and face examples of Jewish men and women embracing faith in Jesus.

Religious issues about salvation and the identity of Jesus puzzle Andrew and Nicodemus. The Samaritan woman, having been married five times and now living with a sixth man, has a problem in her irregular domestic situations.[43] A different family problem affects the royal official; his little son has fallen seriously ill and is at the point of death. A physical disability has condemned an anonymous man to spend his life lying helplessly next to a pool in Jerusalem. When another anonymous person encounters Jesus, she is about to be stoned to death. Martha meets Jesus when she suffers a family tragedy: her beloved brother Lazarus has died. Jesus discloses himself to Mary Magdalene after she has seen him die on the cross and suspects that robbers have taken his body away from the tomb.

Jesus manifests himself to those who suffer from something that affects them personally and often affects their families as well. Some encounter him because they have gone looking for him (Nicodemus and the royal official). One person seemingly blunders into the presence of Jesus (the Samaritan woman). Another is dragged into his presence (the woman caught in adultery). Others encounter Jesus because he himself comes to them (the man born blind). Andrew and his anonymous companion are directed toward Jesus by John the Baptist.

All in all, it does not seem to matter much to the evangelist how Jesus meets these typical figures. The only important thing is that they find themselves in his presence, respond to his initiative, and come to faith.

The Fourth Gospel's narrative of faith displays the passage to faith in Christ, both during his lifetime and after his resurrection from the dead. Andrew, Nicodemus, the Samaritan woman, and the others represent both the first (Jewish) and subsequent (Jewish and Gentile) disciples. The Letter to the Hebrews (11:1—12:2) goes further. It also describes faith as it can be embraced and lived by those who remain "outside" the particular history of Judaism and Christianity. "Faith," we read, "is the assurance of things hoped for, the proof of things not seen. By this [faith] the elders [who include here Noah] received approval [from God]. By faith we understand that this universe was fashioned by the word of God, so that from what cannot be seen that which is seen has come into being" (Heb 11:1–3).[44]

Tradition and Scriptures

Fundamental theology, as the name implies, studies foundational issues. These include: the divine *revelation* communicated through the history of Israel and of Jesus Christ; the conditions that open human beings to the self-communication of God; the nature of *faith* in and through the risen Christ and his Holy Spirit; and the transmission (through the church's *tradition* and *the inspired Scriptures*) of the experience of God's self-communication.

This chapter has presented, albeit fragmentarily, a Christian fundamental theology with an eye on Judaism and Islam. What has been said about divine revelation and human faith can be filled out by what I wrote in *Rethinking Fundamental Theology* (Oxford: Oxford University Press [OUP], 2011) and *Revelation* (OUP, 2016). What should be added (on tradition and the inspired Scriptures) could be gleaned from my *Tradition: Understanding Christian Tradition* (OUP, 2018) and *Inspiration: Towards a Christian Interpretation of Biblical Inspiration* (OUP, 2018). For a preliminary glimpse of what traditions and scriptures embody in Judaism and Islam, I suggest attending worship in a mosque and synagogue. Nothing else promises to let Christians begin experiencing the living traditions and sacred texts of these other two Abrahamic faiths.

Key Themes and Conversation Partners

After fifty years of teaching fundamental theology, I would single out three themes that persistently call for attention. First, the need persists to convince many Catholics and other Christians to follow the lead of the Second Vatican Council in its Constitution on Divine Revelation, *Dei Verbum* (the Word of God) and recognize that revelation is primarily the personal, divine self-disclosure that brings a knowledge *of* God. Secondarily, such foundational self-revelation of God to prophets, apostles, and other official mediators brought a fresh, enlarged knowledge *about* God that would be expressed in propositions, for instance, in the basic creeds. While not primarily propositional, revelation is secondarily "proposition-able."[45]

Second, the need also persists to distinguish firmly between the divine self-revelation and the inspired Scriptures. They record and interpret God's progressive self-disclosure, through Moses, Isaiah, and other mediators, down to those who wrote accounts of the missions of Jesus and the Holy Spirit. Where the Scriptures remain as such written records, revelation is a living encounter with God, which may well be triggered by these texts but is not to be identified with them.

Some Christians insist that "outside the Scriptures there is no revelation" (*extra Scripturam nulla revelatio*). This limits the presence and power of Christ and his Spirit. They are present in a special way through the inspired Scriptures, in the liturgy and lives of the baptized, and through other means. But that fuller presence does not mean an absence elsewhere of revelation and of a call to personal faith, without which it is impossible to please God (Heb 11:6).[46]

Third, a triple timeline characterizes revelation. The prologue to the Letter to the Hebrews announces a past revelation that was perfected and completed: "Long ago God spoke to our ancestors in many and various ways in the prophets, but in these last days he has spoken to us by the Son" (Heb 1:1). This foundational revelation reached its full high point with the coming of Christ and his Spirit.

In dependence on the apostolic generation, later believers experience the divine self-revelation. This ongoing revelation does not add to the essential content of what was fully disclosed in Christ's life, death, and resurrection and the sending of the Holy Spirit. But as a living encounter with Christ through his Spirit, this divine self-communication never stops.

Some New Testament authors follow up Jesus's language about the coming Son of Man (e.g., Mark 13:24–27) by announcing the final manifestation of the glorified Christ at the end of history (e.g., Titus 2:13; Heb 9:28). Paul expects that, when we come to God, "we will see face to face" and "will know fully even as we have been fully known" (1 Cor 13:12).[47] In short, the historical, foundational revelation, like the life-giving revelation here and now, anticipates the definitive self-disclosure of God at the end.

Interlocutors

As regards the *interlocutors* who have challenged, nourished, and helped shape my vision of basic themes of fundamental theology, the largest group are the undergraduates and graduates whom I taught not only in Rome but also throughout the world. They included not only Catholics such as Daniel Harrington, Ormond Rush, and Philip Moller, but also other Christian believers, including George Hunsinger. In the same way not only Catholic fundamental theologians such as Avery Dulles, Jacques Dupuis, René Latourelle, and Jared Wicks but also other Christians such as Henry Chadwick, Sarah Coakley, Stephen Davis, Jürgen Moltmann, and Wolfhart Pannenberg ensured an ecumenical presence of colleagues in my life.

Conversation partners numbered many classical thinkers—such as Aristotle, Plato, Augustine, Anselm, Aquinas, Hume, and Pascal. I welcomed also such modern philosophers as Bloch, Tony Coady, Ryle, and Wittgenstein. Whenever David Braithwaite succeeded in encouraging me to take time out to read what sociologists and other experts in the human sciences said about human tradition and traditions, I found them constantly illuminating. Sad to say, when the Tradition-Scripture issue comes up, too many theologians still remain stuck on the classical debate created by many Catholics (and others) who misunderstood the teaching of the Council of Trent. The Faith and Order Commission of the World Council of Churches, not to mention the Second Vatican Council, laid that debate to rest in the 1960s.[48]

Bible scholars have repeatedly fed my fundamental theology: François Bovon, Raymond Brown, Brendan Byrne, James Dunn, Ulrich Luz, Joel Marcus, and Charles Moule, along with Gerhard von Rad and other German Old Testament commentators. Both in fundamental theology and in the Christology courses I taught and wrote, I set my face against the deficient practice of too many Catholic and other Christian theologians. At times they still relentlessly ignore what the forty-five books of the Old Testament could contribute, books that officially make up well over half of the Christian Bible. I always aimed to incorporate the Jewish books of the Bible as much as possible in the theology I taught and wrote.

Finally, when publishing in fundamental theology took on apologetical characteristics, it produced interesting interlocutors. Apropos of the resurrection of Jesus. I received valuable letters from Géza Vermès (Jewish) and some Christians (e.g., Dale Allison and Dewi Rees). Allison picked up the findings of Rees, the first person to study scientifically bereavement experiences as possibly helpful for understanding encounters with Jesus after his death and resurrection.

Darton, Longman & Todd asked me to write a book in response to Pullman's 2010 work *The Good Man Jesus and the Scoundrel Christ*. Published only a few months after Pullman provocatively retold the story of Jesus on the basis of a twin called "Christ," my *Philip Pullman's Jesus* prompted an interesting article in *The Guardian*, but Pullman himself preferred to respond with total silence.

With an apologetical engagement, this chapter concludes a sketch of Christian fundamental theology as I have practiced it. How this sketch looks from the point of view of Jewish and Islamic theology I leave now to Marc Rastoin and Jean-Marc Balhan.

DIVINE REVELATION ACCORDING TO
CHRISTIANITY, JUDAISM, AND ISLAM

PERSPECTIVE FROM JUDAISM BY MARC RASTOIN

The presentation by Gerald O'Collins rightly emphasizes the importance of friendship in theological thought in general, and in relations between Jews and Christians in particular. Just think of Origen (d. ca. 253) engaged in exchanges with the rabbis of Caesarea, or Rabbi Jonathan Eybeschutz (1690–1764) discussing theology in Prague with his Jesuit friend Franz Haselbauer (1677–1756). Ideas pass through people just like faith itself.

In presenting the thought of Jürgen Moltmann, O'Collins insists on the way in which the thought of this theologian is polarized by the future through rooting itself in Isaiah (see 43:18–19). In fact, Judaism constantly helps Christianity to look to the future, to the return of Christ, and not to lock itself into the past, however glorious. O'Collins reminds us that the New Testament *also* ends with a vigorous call to pray for Christ's return: "Amen! Come, Lord Jesus!" (Rev 22:20b). Christianity strongly celebrates a presence, but it must not forget that it experiences a lack and also lives, sometimes painfully, an absence,[49] an accomplishment ahead of it. We cannot rest on achievements, even if they are religious, but remain stretched toward a Kingdom that we pray will come. We do not expect the *return* of Christ but the *coming* of the Son of Man in glory.

Several times O'Collins recalls the importance of the personal decision of faith, "revelation is primarily personal." Judaism reminds us, on the contrary, that revelation can really be addressed only to a people or a community. An individual faith, or a uniquely personal one, cannot be stated and taught. This is highlighted by the key verse of rabbinic thought: "*We* will do and *we* will listen" (Exod 24:7b). There can be no believing "I" without a "we" that allows and sustains it. There can be no faith accessing a personal formulation without the foundation of community practices allowing it to hatch. O'Collins writes: "revelation is primarily the *personal*, divine self-disclosure that brings a knowledge of God." I would gladly change this to: "revelation is primarily the *communal*, divine self-disclosure that brings a knowledge of God."

This brings us to the question of the incarnation of faith. The paradox is that Christianity, which claims to be a religion of the incarnation, sometimes tends to become disembodied, excessively individualistic, and private, whereas Judaism is deeply rooted in eminently fleshly liturgies and rites. Some recent synods of the Catholic Church, to choose just one example, discuss marriage at length, but, in their conclusions, there is no mention of new liturgical formulas (proper Masses, prefaces, specific penitential rites, and so forth) or of new preparatory rites that take contemporary reality into account. The whole remains very intellectual and disembodied. New translations of the Roman Missal (such as the English version of 2011) have further accentuated the archaic, abstruse, and abstract side of the liturgical texts. Of course, Orthodox Judaism runs this risk. But those who subscribe to it have a very concrete relationship with the language and rites, whereas *Massorti* and liberal Judaisms are engaged in a permanent process of institutional, ritual, and liturgical creativity.

The fundamental novelty of Christianity, as a movement born within Judaism, is to affirm the massive and indisputable coming of the Holy Spirit on all flesh promised by the prophets. For too long Western theology, with its Latin roots, has operated in a pendulum game between Christology and theology (in the strict sense), between the Father and the Son, leaving the Holy Spirit in the shadows. Likewise, Christianity must put the resurrection at the center of its creed as well as its pastoral practice. The two are closely related, as the Spirit is the *life-giving* Spirit.

Jewish theology is quite spontaneously apophatic about God in his person and his mystery. Its focus on *mitzvot* and the commandments can *sometimes* foster a religious life more centered on the legal than on the mystical. But this theology has an advantage, by maintaining the complexity of the character of God. Such theology is not a falsely simple and uniformly sweet aggregate. God is both a demanding and incorruptible judge and a deeply loving and faithful partner, a "God that is both mysteriously other and intimately close," as O'Collins says. This is a God who repents and changes his mind,[50] who accepts contradiction and discussion (see Abraham or Moses in the Torah). To take another example, Benjamin Sommer's investigation of the "bodies of God"[51] opened up new horizons of research that can shed light on the Jewish world of the first century. The absence of dogmatic definitions can prove a great asset, as can the incessant rabbinical ability to privilege the question over the answer, the lived experience over the intellectual, and the concrete over the abstract.

Thus the Jewish way of life, even more than its theology and its propositional content, invites Christianity to awaken its eschatological consciousness, to embody the Spirit who makes it live in communal as well as personal liturgies and rites, to constantly explore again and again its origins and the sources of its most decisive theological concepts: the Messiah, the Son of Man, the resurrection, the Holy Spirit, and the eschatology grafted upon history.

PERSPECTIVE FROM ISLAM BY JEAN-MARC BALHAN

"We never forget our first love," Gerald O'Collins declares at the opening of his preface: from the beginning of his academic career, fundamental theology "sparked his first love." He was faithful to it all his life, in dialogue with many scholars from various disciplines and religious traditions who shared similar passions.

I experienced something similar when, as a young Jesuit, I was sent as a teacher to Egypt in the early 1990s, a foundational experience that determined the rest of my life. I was living for the first time in my life among Muslims, to the rhythm of the muezzin's calls proclaiming five times a day: "God is greater. I testify that there is no god but God." It was an opportunity to realize that God is always "greater" (*semper maior*) than the narrow images we have of him. These last three decades spent in the company of Muslims have been for me, in the mirror of their gaze and their tradition, a time of "decanting" that has allowed God to make himself ever more "visible" to my eyes. The "transforming I-thou" at work in the relationship with God of which O'Collins speaks is realized in the concrete existence of a person—in close connection with all the "I-thou transforming" that operates within the relationships in which his life is woven.

In Cairo, the atmosphere resonates not only with the call to prayer, but also with the Qur'anic recitation, constantly broadcast in the stalls lining the streets of the city. Chanted according to precise rules in a unique language, it fascinates those who pay attention to it: the believers who hear God speak to them today as in the time of the Prophet; the aesthetes seduced by its mysterious beauty; or the theologians or seekers of God wishing to better understand "how God speaks" and "what he says."

O'Collins talks about "means, mediators and mystery of revelation." In Sunni Islam, we *hear* the Word of God, through the mediation of the Prophet and that of all those who have successively memorized and recited it over the centuries, until today. This memorization, recitation, and hearing ensure the proximity of a presence while at the same time preserving the distance of transcendence. After hearing this Word, the believer responds by his testimony to God's Oneness and obedience to his commandments.

If the accounts of the ascension of the Prophet make us contemplate the seven heavens and their inhabitants, and if some even relate that the Prophet could have seen God, the Qur'an is clear on this subject: no one can *see* God (Q 6:103: "No vision can take Him in, but He takes in all vision"), except on the day of the Resurrection (Q 75:22–23): "On that Day there will be radiant faces, looking towards their Lord."[47] To Moses, who had asked him for permission to see him, God replied:

> "You will never see Me, but look at that mountain: if it remains standing firm, you will see Me," and when his Lord manifested Himself to the mountain, He made it crumble: Moses fell down unconscious. When he recovered, he said, "Glory be to You! To You I turn in repentance! I am the first to believe!" He said, "Moses, I have raised you above other people by [giving you] My messages and speaking to you: hold on to what I have given you; be one of those who give thanks." (Q 7:143–44)

Of God, we can see only the signs he grants us. But even in this case, it is not primarily a question of perception but of recognition of what is communicated to us by these signs, to which the believer is invited to respond by a profession of faith in the Divine Oneness and by obedience to his commandments. One can therefore "see" and be blind: as O'Collins points out, no revelation without faith and vice versa.

"Christian, Jewish, and Muslim believers accept a personal God who has entered into a self-revealing relationship," O'Collins affirms. In what way does God reveal "himself" in Islam? Muslims revere the Prophet in a special way and their devotion leads them to exalt and imitate his external and inner beauty. He is not, however, the "face of God" because, properly speaking, God has no "face." As we have said and repeated, it is through signs, in creation, in history and, last but not least, in Scripture, that he reveals himself. If he brings down from heaven Scripture, rain, and other graces, he himself does not come down.

Muslim mysticism rejects everything that could suggest an incarnation (*hulûl*) of God or a substantial union (*ittihâd*) between God and humanity. In Sufism, "mystical union" takes the form of a "substitution" in which the personality of God's friend is "vanished," like the moth ignited by the flame of a candle, to quote an image taken from the Sufis. This dissolution of self-consciousness (*fanâ'*) is the most radical proclamation of divine oneness (*tawhîd*), which the Sufi can only receive by "disappearing" himself, without having any part in it. As the Persian mystic Ansârî states (d. 1089):

> No one really testifies to God that He is One, since anyone who imagines doing so denies Him. The attestation of those who utter such an epithet is only a vain sentence nullified by the One. Only God testifies to his Oneness! Whoever speaks of it deserves the epithet of atheist.[48]

This experience is regarded by Sufis as a return to the state that was that of human beings during pre-eternity, in the course of the primordial Covenant, when they were still mysteriously in God (Q 7:172). The experience of passionate love in which the lover forgets himself in the beloved, particularly developed in literature (think of the story of Majnûn and Laylâ), provides a parable of this. The nostalgia provoked in the heart of the Sufi by hearing the reed flute will provide another parable, as Rûmî tells us in the poem introducing his *Mathnawî*. O'Collins said: "We never forget our first love": neither does the Sufi.

Above creation, separated from it, God does not come down. The One, transcendent, is like nothing. At the same time, he is at work in

DIVINE REVELATION ACCORDING TO CHRISTIANITY, JUDAISM, AND ISLAM

the world and in history, where his traces can be seen, and he is "closer to [man] than his jugular vein" (Q 50:16). The Qur'an also describes him without being afraid to use anthropomorphisms and reveals his "Names,"[49] and these will be an important object of study for dialectical theology (*'ilm al-kalâm*), questioning the status of God's attributes within the framework of this strict monotheism. These Names are also an important mediation of the Muslim's prayer: their repetition in the Qur'an shapes the representation of God of the believer who has at heart to memorize them, recite them, meditate on them, and invoke God with them as invited by Q 7:180, which says: "The Most Excellent Names belong to God: use them to call on Him." To do this, believers use a rosary of ninety-nine beads corresponding to the ninety-nine Names of God, according to the famous *hadith* that assigns them this number: "God has ninety-nine Names—one hundred minus one—and whoever keeps them in memory will enter paradise."

Finally, one cannot speak of God's self-revelation in Islam without quoting the *hadith qudsî* in which God expresses so well his desire to reveal himself: "I was a hidden treasure, and I wanted to be known. That is why I created the world, to be known in it." From this *hadith*, Ibn 'Arabî (d. 1240) will develop a particular way of conceiving monotheism in Islam. For him, the world becomes what could be called a "theophany," where created beings have only relative existence, as a manifestation of divine Names.[50]

2

"SO NEAR AND YET SO FAR"

How Do Jews Do Theology?

Marc Rastoin, SJ

TO SPEAK OF "Jewish theology" is challenging for two reasons. First, the word *theology* does not have an exact equivalent in Judaism, which means we have to delve into the traditional Jewish way of conceiving the "things of God." Second, what does the term *Judaism* mean? The Greek term *ioudaismos* is found in Paul (Gal 1:13; see 2 Macc 2:21), but it was not really used by Jews until the nineteenth century. What is more, it usually designates so-called rabbinic Judaism, derived from the Babylonian Talmud and patiently elaborated by a community of sages between the second and sixth centuries. But many Jewish thinkers and communities have challenged, more or less directly, this religious "model,"[1] preferring instead to speak of people, community, or even family.[2]

Preliminary Observations

There are today three main ways of considering the question of the relationship between early Christianity and those Jews who did not accept Jesus as Messiah (and as consubstantial with the divinity). First, some see a strong, fundamental continuity between Judaism before the destruction of the Second Temple in 70 CE and rabbinic Judaism, which followed in particular the party of the Pharisees. This is the traditional view of the Jewish religious world, which traces the conceptual elaboration of the Talmud back to Ezra, as the famous verse from the Maxims of the Fathers puts it: "Moses received the Torah on Sinai and delivered it to Joshua, and Joshua delivered it to the elders, and the elders to the prophets, and the prophets delivered it to the men of the Great Synagogue. They said three things: be patient in justice, raise many disciples and make a fence round the Torah" (*Pirkei Avot* 1.1).

Curiously, however, the Talmud speaks very little of the Pharisees—and only then to criticize them, attributing the fall of the second temple to the hatred and divisions within the Jewish people before 70 CE, including the Pharisees (*Talmud Bavli*, *Yoma* 9b). This way of understanding the sequence of events tends to underestimate the importance of Hellenistic Judaism, which flourished for several centuries, notably in the key period at the beginning of the common era. Philo of Alexandria is seen by some as the thinker who could reasonably lay claim to having been one of the greatest "theologians" of Judaism. His way of dealing with Greek philosophy anticipates in some respects the work of the church fathers (many of whom read him) and Jewish thinkers of the Middle Ages who also read Aristotle.

A second way of considering the relationship between Christianity and Judaism that has become increasingly popular in recent years is to see them as "twin brothers,"[3] which has the disadvantage of seeing them as "-isms" (via a quite dogmatic theological reading). They are thus perceived as the two surviving "branches" emerging from second-temple Judaism (bearing in mind that the Essenian or Qumranian strand disappeared after 70 CE just as the party of the Sadducees did). There is some truth in this approach, but it also seems somewhat contrived: the conflicts were more about questions of practice than about points of belief.[4]

A third approach sees in "Judaism" a religion that *postdates* Christianity.[5] In historical terms the approach is attractive because rabbinic Judaism in and of itself is undoubtedly established *after* the birth of the Christian movement—and it is true that the hermeneutical logic that leads to the constitution of the Babylonian Talmud and the Justinian Code is analogous and contemporary. Nevertheless, like most scholars, I see more continuity between the end of "biblical" religion and Judaism. And I would argue that this provocative approach rests on fragile historical hypotheses and has significant risks for Christian thought. Today all theologians or historians of religion are conscious of the dangers posed by too hastily using concepts that seem to be clear and universal but that in reality have a complex history and constitute filters for approaching a less tangible reality.

While it is important to realize, in John Henry Newman's sense of the term, the very difficult translation of theological concepts derived from the Christian tradition (such as grace, sin, redemption, sacrament, and creed) to speak of Jewish religious thought, it is also important not to neglect two fundamental elements. First, every "religion" or philosophical system addresses humanity's fundamental existential questions: Is there a God or not? Are we free or not?[6] What is the origin of evil, and how is it to be effectively fought against? Did God reveal himself under a given name or not? In inspired writings or not? These questions are fundamentally common to Jewish and Christian thought, and, notwithstanding the differences in overall framing and terminology, the similarities are sometimes bigger than generally thought—such as those concerning "original sin" and the "inclination to do evil" (the *yetser harah*), or the Holy Spirit, for example. And there is also the fact that a significant proportion of the textual material is identical, even if it is read differently.[7]

Second, Jewish religious thought of the past two millennia has developed largely in a context shaped by Christianity and the exchange of ideas between the two traditions. Following other contemporary thinkers, Daniel Boyarin has rightly drawn our attention to the limitations of such terms as *borrowings* or *influences*, which are so commonly used in the cultural domain, because they imply that there is such a thing as the *essence* of Christianity or Judaism; that sometimes, under certain circumstances, bridges are built between them; and that we are dealing here with autonomous traditions that only occasionally and accidentally intersect. Instead, Boyarin argues, it is more helpful to draw on the concept of shared cultural *matrices* or *hybridization*.[8] No religion is an island—and this has been so since the beginning of time. Moses Maimonides no doubt has more in common with, say, Thomas Aquinas than with Philo a thousand years earlier.[9] Greek philosophy fed in profound ways the two religious communities, and second-temple Judaism was itself already an eminently Hellenistic religion.[10]

Judaism is, therefore, fundamentally plural in its very long temporality and very varied in its expressions across different cultural and geographical spheres. The contrast between Arabic-language Judaism in Yemen and nineteenth-century German Judaism is a case in point. This has led some to speak of "Judaisms" in the plural.[11] And yet all these currents converge in a strong, shared identity, often more *genealogical* than strictly *religious*, that sees them as *am Israel*, the people or community of Israel, sharing the same sacred language, the same inspired writings, the same fundamental rites (circumcision, Sabbath, *kashrut*, and *niddah*), the same passion for Jerusalem and the land of Israel, even if the "Zionist" dimension—however anachronistic that term—has varied considerably over time.[12] Thus the concept of *Ahavat Israel*—love for the community of Israel—will unite almost all Jewish groups (with the exception of a small number of marginal sects). The collective sense of belonging to an indissolubly ethnic and religious human reality—which is always hard for a Christian to understand[13]—is strong, including among people who have little faith and follow few strictly "religious" or cultural practices.

Jewish Tradition

These opening observations, while long, are important if we are to avoid making of "Judaism" a sort of abstract, atemporal essence. What then is the central principle, if it can be identified, of the Jewish tradition? A classic and still quite relevant approach is to see in the Jewish tradition a radically "orthopractic" tradition where collective *conduct* counts for more than orthodoxy or individual *faith*.[14] This is a tradition that very much emphasizes communal rituals, be they within the family or in the synagogue. The key verse underpinning this strong insistence on *action* is the people's response to Moses as he presents the Torah on Mount Sinai: "We will do and we will listen," or *naassé venishma* (Exod 24:7). From a cultural and Christian point of view, the word order is paradoxical, the reader generally expecting to reverse the order of the verbs, placing understanding *before* action. Instead, the idea emphasized here is that it is from doing that entering into communication with the divine flows: in short, faith is born from action.

In this context the ritualistic commandments, which appear unjustifiable in rational or ethical terms, are just as important in religious terms as the ethical commandments (in the Ten Commandments, for instance). The weight attached to ritual practice distinguishes Jewish ways of thinking from one another and from those of Christians (who by and large do not keep the ritual commandments).[15]

In liberal or Masorti Judaism, concessions to modernity are allowed that Orthodox rabbis condemn. However, it is also the case that the *Halakhah*, while trying to ensure continuity in different circumstances, has constantly evolved throughout history. In the face of the challenge posed by modernity, differences have emerged over the nature and extent of any concessions to be made, with a conservative pole and a modernist pole—and a whole range of positions in between.

In rabbinic Judaism there is an absolute coherence between the written Torah, *Torah she-bi-khtav*, and the oral Torah, *Torah she-be-'al peh*, transcribed in the Babylonian Talmud.[16] More specifically,

DIVINE REVELATION according to CHRISTIANITY, JUDAISM, and ISLAM

the same religious authority is expected to be given to the rabbinical, oral tradition as it is to the written text of the Hebrew Bible.[17] Tradition and Scripture are inseparable. This point has always been called into question, beginning with the Sadducees, whom we know through Flavius Josephus and the New Testament, and followed by the powerful movement of the Karaites. In the seventh to ninth centuries, they threatened the supremacy of rabbinic Judaism.[18] And it has to be noted that, for later religious authorities, the authority of the Talmud can even supplant that of the biblical text.[19] This can be seen, for example, in the case of a man's obligation to take a second wife if his first is sterile.[20]

The Talmud is an immense collection of discussions and decisions about how the commandments deriving from the biblical text are to be lived out in daily life. Christian readers can be surprised to see different opinions often being expressed—and at some length—in the Talmud. But ultimately *one* way of doing things is insisted upon. That said, rabbis and other decision-makers are still active today in determining what exactly are the limits of the divine commandments and how they are to be put into practice. And they often disagree. This activity necessarily takes up much more space than the discussion of "abstract" theological themes.[21] But these themes are treated in a more diffuse and open way.

Traditionally a distinction is made within the corpus between the *Halakhah* and the *Aggadah*: the former focuses on the "how" and the rituals, while the latter focuses on everything else, including what Christians call theology. In a sense, the *Halakhah* is unified (even if the Talmud does not systematically take a clear line) whereas the *Aggadah* is diverse. The *Aggadah* can contain an element of moral exhortation or an emphasis on certain of God's attributes, but it can also contain folklore, various pieces of advice, or parables. One of the most popular compilations of Aggadic materials, derived from the Babylonian Talmud, is the *Eyn Yaakov*, put together by Jacob ibn Habib in the sixteenth century.[22] It follows, then, that theological discourse is fragmentary and in narrative form, embracing both real plurality and fundamental unity, belief always being the foundation for actions (ritual or moral).

It can therefore be argued that the element of systematic doctrinal teaching, which has, at least since the Middle Ages, been a defining characteristic of Christianity, is not emphasized in the same way in the Jewish tradition, which instead focuses on the legal aspect. The "theological" teachings are numerous, rich, and, I would argue, fundamentally coherent, even if they have different emphases, but they are scattered in an apparently almost random way across the Talmud, with no attempt made to establish a hierarchy of articles of faith or restrictive definitions. One very famous exception, which is found in most of the Jewish prayer books (*siddourim*), is the *Thirteen Principles of Faith* formulated by the twelfth-century Jewish philosopher Moses Maimonides, also known as the Rambam, one of the greatest Jewish religious thinkers of all time.[23] In a sense his *Guide of the Perplexed* is a work of fundamental "theology," even if it can also be seen as a work of philosophy.[24]

From Moses Maimonides to Abraham Heschel

Maimonides sought to offer a succinct account of the heart of Jewish faith. The first five articles are about God: (1) he is the creator and master of all; (2) he is one, "in a Unity like no other"; (3) he is incorporeal;[25] (4) he is beyond time and creation; and (5) he alone is worthy to receive prayers.[26] The next four articles concern (6) the truth of biblical prophecy; (7) the preeminence of Moses, "father of all the Prophets, both those before and those after him"; (8) the integrity of the Torah as it has been received; and (9) the immutability of the Torah. The next two articles are about the much-debated question of freedom of will and justice, focusing on (10) God's omniscience and (11) God's justice and therefore his judgment. For he "rewards those who follow his commandments and punishes those who transgress them." And the last two articles move to the heart of the Christian faith: (12) the coming of the Messiah and (13) the resurrection of the dead. Although many Jewish thinkers—from the twelfth century to the present day—have argued that Maimonides goes too far on the question of the coming of the Messiah, having himself been, in his letter to the Yemenites, somewhat skeptical about excessively enthusiastic messianic expectations,[27] his formulation has remained famous: "I believe with perfect faith in the coming of the Messiah, and even if he delays, I will wait every day for him to come." The last principle—symbolically the thirteenth, beyond the limit of twelve—declares: "I believe with perfect faith that there will be a resurrection of the dead at the time chosen by the Creator, that His name is blessed and that the remembrance of Him will be exalted forever and for all eternity." The tension present in Maimonides's works between an incorporeal, even philosophical conception of the resurrection and the biblical verses evoking its corporeal nature is a tension that also runs through the Christian tradition.

Despite criticisms of them, Maimonides's principles still offer today a good starting point and an elegant and sober summary of the heart of Jewish faith. But they do so, interestingly, without explicitly mentioning the historical event that is at the heart of the cultural and spiritual experience of Israel, namely, the exodus from Egypt. That said, the prophet Moses occupies the central position in Maimonides in the same way that Jesus does in the Christian creed. For, as Robert Jenson notes, "God is whoever raised Jesus from the dead, having before raised Israel from Egypt."[28] The resurrection of Christ is to Christian faith what the exodus from Egypt is to Jewish faith. Just as the Christian lives alongside, as it were, the Messiah at every Easter and at every Eucharist, so the Jew must also think of themselves, at the Passover *seder*, as having *themselves* left Egypt.

This radical preeminence of legal discussions about the commandments, with the resultant insistence on the proper form of reasoning,[29] has often given rise to mystical revolts. However, it is worth noting that mystical, devotional, and liturgical inflections were not, on the whole, antinomic but, rather, expressed a search for meaning and for poetry (*piyyoutim*). During the first rabbinical era, synagogue leaders or Jewish sages tried to oppose the rabbis of the Talmud. The high Middle Ages (eleventh–fourteenth centuries)—an extraordinary intellectual and spiritual golden age—saw the rise of *Kabbalah*, which reached its peak with thinkers such as Moses Cordovero (1522–72) and Isaac Luria (1534–72), and which emphasized mysticism, the esoteric dimension of prayer, and religious emotions.[30]

In the seventeenth century, there emerged in eastern Europe, similarly, a current that is still very much alive today, namely, Hasidism. Reacting against the despair felt by persecuted Jewish communities and the intellectual poverty of rabbinical schools of his day, Israel Ben Eliezer (1698–1760), the Baal Shem Tov ("The Master of the Good Name"), created a new form of piety emphasizing the importance of joy and the emotions in the mystical experience and gathered around him several disciples. Despite the bitter opposition of rivals, known appropriately as the *mitnagdim* ("opponents"), the movement grew and, despite the awful losses inflicted on them by the Nazis during the Holocaust, still thrives today. Its members follow a ritual practice that is similar to—and in some ways more rigorous than—that of other Orthodox Jews, with the result that tensions are today far less strong than they were in the eighteenth century, though by no means nonexistent. Indeed, an irresolvable tension runs throughout Jewish religious history between rationalism and legalism on the one hand and, on the other, mysticism and piety, as we shall see later.

Almost all Jewish communities up until the time of the French Revolution belonged to the traditional rabbinical world. Those Jews who left this rabbinical world did so by conversion—either forced (as in 1492 in Spain and in 1496 in Portugal) or voluntary—to integrate themselves into the majority Christian society.[31] As Jews—gradually and not without opposition—became full citizens of the majority of European countries, the traditional community-based model that had shaped the Jewish world for generations began to fragment.

DIVINE REVELATION ACCORDING TO CHRISTIANITY, JUDAISM, AND ISLAM

That unbelievable resilience of the rabbinic world, which was yet so vulnerable, has been praised by the important religious Israeli thinker Yeshayahou Leibowitz:

> It is necessary to reverse the question. The question is not how Judaism collapsed during the last generations. But how did it last over twenty-four generations? That is the great mystery. It is an historical phenomenon without parallel. How did the Jewish people accept the burden of the Torah and of the *mitzvot* without any power, any force of the political setting obliging them to do so?[32]

But the nineteenth century saw the undoing of this world that, despite external pressures and internal dissensions, had been firmly held together by shared practice.

Reform Judaism was born, borrowing certain liturgical forms from German Protestantism. The question posed by Reform Judaism is how to reconcile tradition and the modern world—or, how to maintain the traditional faith while taking account of the ideas raised by the *Haskalah*, the Jewish Enlightenment.[33] Thinkers associated with this movement entered into intellectual dialogue with the major Christian philosophers and theologians—and the famous Judeo-German synthesis proved to be rich indeed. While some Jews, assimilated into the dominant culture, became nominally Christian or of no religion at all, many chose to remain as Jews while completely rethinking their place in the Jewish religious world. Instructive in this respect are Franz Rosenzweig's landmark study *The Star of Redemption* (1921)[34] and that of his friend Martin Buber, *I and Thou* (1923), which had a major influence on twentieth-century Christian theology and philosophy.[35] In parallel, faced with this challenge, the world centered on the faithful practice of the commandments became more entrenched, giving rise to what is known as "Orthodox Judaism"—a subtly ironic title—which set itself the task of maintaining the classical, rabbinical priority of orthopraxy. Later this was to evolve further still with the founding of "Modern Orthodox Judaism" under the influence of Rabbi Joseph Soloveitchik (1903–93) and various disciples who incorporated to different degrees the values of modernity, such as equality of the sexes and interreligious dialogue.[36]

There is no shortage of great Jewish religious thinkers in the twentieth century—among them, Shaul Lieberman (1898–1983), Emmanuel Levinas (1905–85), Louis Jacobs (1920–2006), Léon Ashkenazi (1922–96), David Weiss Halivni (1927–2022), Michael Wyschogrod (1928–2015), and Jonathan Sacks (1948–2020)—but few of them have articulated any kind of global "theological" synthesis.

The exception here is Abraham Joshua Heschel (1907–72), who, in addition to his well-known work on the place of the Sabbath in the Jewish faith,[37] published *Torah min Hashamaim*, an in-depth account of the major tensions in the Jewish tradition.[38] It is worth noting that this way of presenting a profile of a religious and theological tradition, highlighting the structural tensions running through it, makes one think of the theological work of the Jesuit scholar Erich Przywara.[39]

Heschel's most important insight is that since the time of the earliest rabbis—the *Tannaim*—the Jewish tradition has been animated by a fruitful tension between the rationalist and sober approach of Rabbi Yishmael and the more mystical and lyrical approach of Rabbi Akiva. There was, to be sure, a difference in tone between these two second-century sages, but Heschel sees in this difference the key to understanding all the subsequent debates in Jewish theological history. Through this dichotomy he casts new light on all the great theological debates—about the creation of the world and redemption, about free will and the freedom of God, about the struggle between divine justice and divine mercy—and in so doing he rehabilitates the *Aggadah* in relation to the *Halakhah*.

In her introduction, Heschel's daughter Susannah Heschel presented thus those two great polarities: "For him, the school of

DIVINE REVELATION ACCORDING TO
CHRISTIANITY, JUDAISM, AND ISLAM

Akiva was mystical, apocalyptic, radical, uncompromising, enthusiastic, strong, militant, deep, paradoxical, and sweeping, whereas the school of Ishmael was critical, rationalistic, self-limited, clear, dry, measured, balanced, careful, and patient." Heschel was a man of equilibrium, and he feared a Judaism in which the school of Akiba would have eliminated that of Yishmael. For him, rather, the two should be maintained so that the faith remains in a state of permanent and fruitful tension: "Everything cycles in the world; and just as the intellectual problems remain with us, so does the tension. The divergences and dissensions between the two 'fathers of the world' continued on their way throughout the generations." He goes on to eulogize intellectually Yishmael, whom he often seems to prefer—without going so far as to neglect the genius and, even in a certain way, the necessity of Akiba:

> What were Rabbi Ishmael's personal characteristics? Delicacy, intellectual reserve, clear thinking, and sobriety. He sought the middle way, and his words were carefully measured. His emotional equilibrium and his intellectual sobriety did not allow his feelings to sweep him off into extremism. He preferred one small, immaculate measure of understanding to nine measures of extremism; one small measure of lucidity to nine measures of profundity. Paradox was anathema to him, and he expended his energy on clarity and precision, on that which was given to understanding and cognition.

But that is not to say that Heschel neglects the genius of Akiva:

> Rabbi Akiva could be credited with seeking out the wondrous. Rabbi Yishmael could be credited with shunning the wondrous. He shook no structural beams; nor did he impose his authority on the text. Among his good qualities was a level-headed caution. Better in his eyes was a single

> measure of reflection on what is written and given than massive speculation above and beyond the very limits of apprehension. One who sees Rabbi Yishmael in a dream should "anticipate wisdom." Rabbi Yishmael's teachings contain straightforward logic, and with it lucidity, simplicity of language, and an aversion to intellectual games. Attributions to him have no superfluity of language or florid expressions. He sought to strip Scripture of anthropomorphisms and to excise unnecessary metaphor and imagery. But Rabbi Akiva's teachings sought to penetrate to inner depths with profundity and potency of language. He did not shrink from anthropomorphism, but rather he preserved the concrete in Scripture, cherished imaginative meanings, added metaphorical embellishments, and created images of the supernal world. Instead of a logic that was subservient to surface meaning, he championed free exegesis and intellectual flights. A poet at heart, and at the same time a razor-sharp genius, Rabbi Akiva was special in that two fundamental qualities were combined in him: poetry and acuity, the esoteric and the analytic.[40]

Reason and poetry, restraint, and passion, the absolute of God and respect for all human beings: all these must go hand in hand.

What is more, Heschel's analysis of the traditional debates running through the Jewish tradition serves to remind us that, while they can seem far removed from Christian *disputationes*, those debates are often similar to the tensions that are also consubstantial to Christianity. The polarity between, on the one hand, rational, philologically informed exegesis that has nothing of the mystical about it and, on the other, spiritual exegesis, discovering Christ in all things, is as old as biblical theology itself, even if scholars tend—no doubt too simplistically—to situate it under the aegis of the debate between the more allegorical school of Alexandria and the more grammatical school of Antioch. The Christian theologian would do well to reflect on these tensions: fundamentally, they are no more erasable in the Christian tradition than they are in the Jewish tradition.

By showing that faith should be translated more into actions than into pious feelings; by championing as a point of principle intelligence and discussion; by having an organic conception of the good of the community of Israel as having primacy over purely intellectual controversies; and by living the permanent unity between the biblical text and the always living tradition that translates it into everyday life, Judaism opens up to the Christian theologian a world that casts light both on the intellectual and spiritual journey of Jesus of Nazareth and on what is possible for faith in a secular world that increasingly corrodes the idea of an historical revelation founded on a divine choice. Judaism offers the Christian theologian a strangeness that is sufficiently familiar to shake their theology out of a misplaced tranquility. It will always be worthwhile to delve into the world of the Jewish tradition.

PERSPECTIVE FROM CHRISTIANITY BY GERALD O'COLLINS

From the point of view of Christian fundamental theology, Marc Rastoin's chapter presents much food for thought and, indeed, challenges for action. His preliminary observations list some major existential questions faced by every religious thinker, and not least by Christian and Jewish scholars alike.

From such broader considerations, he turns particular when suggesting that the classic text by Moses Maimonides, *Guide of the Perplexed*, could also be seen as a work of "fundamental theology." When I taught fundamental theology at the Gregorian University in Rome (1973–2006), this comment would have prompted me to look for a doctoral student interested in and capable of verifying in detail Rastoin's statement. It may also have made Maimonides one of the authors to be studied in fundamental theology.

What Rastoin wrote has also brought me a proposal that should have been investigated but, as far as I know, has never been taken up. Christian theologians have debated the relationship between the inspired Scriptures and the living tradition, while sometimes sadly ignoring the ways in which they were inseparable, being united in their origin (the historical divine self-revelation), functions in everyday life, and future goal (the final vision of God). Should these debates have been illuminated by introducing analogous Jewish discussions of the religious authority to be attributed to the oral traditions and to the written text of the Bible? There may well be comparative studies that took up this issue. But as a Christian fundamental theologian, I feel deprived by never having benefited from them.

Rastoin ends with a statement that is patently true and helpful: "it will always be worthwhile to delve into the world of the Jewish tradition," or, as we might put it, "the world of Jewish traditions." Such research can be particularly worthwhile for Christian fundamental theologians.

DIVINE REVELATION ACCORDING TO CHRISTIANITY, JUDAISM, AND ISLAM

A few years ago I published *Tradition: Understanding Christian Tradition*,[41] motivated in large part by the current failure of many theologians to take up the transmission of God's self-manifestation. Examples of this neglect are not hard to come by: for instance, the long and in many ways admirable *New Dictionary of Theology*.[42] This large dictionary (1,144 pages) contains no entry on "tradition," and does not even list *tradition* in its index. Some knowledge of and concern for the long-standing Jewish debates on the relationship between the biblical text and the lived tradition that translates it into everyday life would have benefited Christian theologians and inhibited their neglect of tradition.

The historical information provided by Rastoin illustrates abundantly the role of tradition in guiding the spiritual journey of the community of Israel. In studying this, Christian theologians might also seek help from sociologists who have advanced our appreciation of tradition. It was no accident that the modern sociologist who authored the most acclaimed work in this area was Jewish: Edward Shils of the University of Chicago.[43]

In recent years memory studies, which often heavily overlap with studies in the area of tradition, have enriched us, in particular by work on tradition as collective memory.[44] The relevance of these findings to what Rastoin, along with Jean-Marc Balhan and myself, have set ourselves to investigate is clear. Right in his opening paragraph, Rastoin reminded readers that Jewish thinkers and communities preferred to speak of "people, community and even family." The traditions they transmitted were obviously understood to be social and embedded in the collective memory.

Insights from studies of collective memory, undertaken by sociologists and other scholars, promise to throw further light on the functions of Jewish as well as Christian memory or tradition. Up to the fairly recent past, sociologists and similar experts tended to take a negative view of collective memory. As Barry Schwartz puts it, "believing all realities to be socially constructed, a generation of scholars depreciated collective memory." Schwartz and some more recent authors have rejected the blanket view that collective memory (or tradition) *merely* reconstructs the past, adapts historical facts to the beliefs and spiritual needs of the present, or even creates such "facts." Rather, he argues that as "an intrinsic part of culture, collective memory works in tandem with science, politics, religion, art, and common sense to interpret experience."[45]

Beyond question, memory, collective or otherwise, is invariably and inevitably selective, simplified, and structured; it can be consciously manipulated and frequently lapses into forgetfulness. Nevertheless, in various ways it also operates under the constraints of history. Memory reflects as well as shapes social reality. Its claims to represent the past faithfully may not be dismissed out of hand. There is some legitimacy to the historical knowledge carried by collective memory or tradition.

Recent memory studies (coming from such scholars as Paul Connerton, James Fentress, Paul Ricœur, Barry Schwartz, and Chris Wickham) can encourage us to apply to Christian and Jewish tradition the scholarly conclusions about the nature and role of collective (or social) memory. Collective memory can perform a properly systematic role in uniting and clarifying various aspects of Christian and Jewish views of tradition.[46]

Some Christian theologies of tradition have followed Yves Congar by (briefly) describing tradition as the collective memory of the church. Yet Joseph Ratzinger, George H. Tavard, and J.-M.-R. Tillard, like Congar, seemingly remained unaware of the development of studies about memory (and forgetting) in anthropology, history, neuroscience, philosophy, psychology, and sociology. Scriptural scholars have happily drawn on modern memory studies. But theologians, almost universally, have failed to incorporate those studies and take advantage of insights that could illuminate and enrich reflection on tradition.

Rastoin ends his chapter with several Jewish convictions that should open up for Christian theologians major realities: the significance of faith in the divine revelation for the good of the community; "the always living tradition," which translates "the biblical text into everyday life"; and, in general, "a strangeness that is sufficiently familiar to shake their theology out of a misplaced tranquility." The challenge should no longer be neglected and could contribute to a new spring in a major area of Christian fundamental theology.

PERSPECTIVE FROM ISLAM BY JEAN-MARC BALHAN

In his chapter, Gerald O'Collins says, "As a Christian I shrink from treating the Jewish faith among 'the other religions.'" In his, Marc Rastoin addresses the question of the links between Judaism and Christianity, from the beginning of course but also in the Middle Ages. Here he rightly says: "Maimonides probably has more in common with a Thomas Aquinas than with a Philo a millennium earlier." Finally, he addresses this question when he examines the encounter between Judaism and modernity. But where is Islam, which also claims to be the "religion of Abraham" (Q 2:135)? Does it have no place in this relationship? Wouldn't the relationship between Judaism and Christianity sometimes be a bit "fusional"? What place for the Islamic third?

On the one hand, in the course of history, these three traditions intellectually interacted with one another: originally of course, but also later in the Arab world in which they first lived together and shared the same language. In the Middle Ages in the Aristotelian epistemological framework that they had in common, these interactions gave rise to major works: Thomas Aquinas debated the thought of Averroes and his contemporary Maimonides, who read Avicenna and Ghazâlî.[52] On the other hand, it is true that Islam comes "after" its two predecessors whom it claims to "correct" in a somewhat "irritating" way for them (as Christianity had earlier done for Judaism). The formation of "Christendom" and later of "Europe" constituted Islam into the "Other" by which they define themselves. The arrival of modernity broke the Aristotelian epistemological framework that was common to them; and finally, the political and ideological evolutions that follow (colonization, Zionism, nationalism, "fundamentalisms" of all kinds, and so forth) further increase the distance.

Rastoin rightly mentions the importance of the concepts of a common cultural matrix or cross-hybridization. In this context, for example, it is interesting to note that current research that situates the Qur'an as a text of late antiquity invites us to reconsider the place of Islam theologically and historically in relation to the biblical tradition and the intellectual history of what will become Europe in this period.[53] As for Muslim-Christian dialogue, it has experienced several turning points over the last fifty years: after an unconditional commitment on the Catholic side followed by a phase of skepticism, a third stage seems to be opening after the Regensburg speech of Pope Benedict XVI (2006), marked by the Muslim initiative of dialogue.[54] While in recent decades, in several parts of the world, Muslim thinkers have entered modernity on the same level,[55] we can perhaps hope for fruitful encounters between us.

On another question, which concerns the notion of "Judaism," Rastoin notes that Jews prefer to speak of "people, community, even family" rather than using "a religious model." To define what all Jews have in common beyond their differences, he evokes an identity "often more genealogical than properly religious." It is interesting to note that from the beginning, the Qur'an aims to "dissolve" genealogical relations,[56] first in opposition to the customs of the Arabs who find honor and security in them. Thus the Qur'an states (49:13): "In God's eyes, the most honored of you are the ones most mindful of Him." On the day of judgment, tribe, clan, family, relationships, sources of security and prestige, will not be able to do anything for the one to be judged (Q 80:33–37; Q 70:8–14): to pass the test, one must move to an ethic based on individual responsibility, where the object of charity are the poor and the stranger (Q 90:1–20).

Then, the Qur'an also stands in contradiction to the Jewish notion of "chosen people." Genealogical relationships must be replaced by a spiritual relationship. Here, the Abraham of the Book of Jubilees serves as a model, he who destroyed the idols of his clan and was then rejected by his relatives (Q 37:83–99) and then established a new genealogy spiritually rooted in God. In Q 37:99–111, the story continues with Abraham's sacrifice, which once again puts the spiritual bond with God above the family bond. In the Qur'anic version of this account, the son's name is not mentioned, the blessing Abraham receives at the end is personal to him, and his descendants through Isaac have no privileges: "some of their offspring were good, but some clearly wronged themselves" (Q 37:113).

Witnessing to the one God and obeying his commandments is more important than family relationships. Thus, in the Qur'an, after the Hegira, the Meccan believers, allied with the Medinans, will use a violence that could be called "religious" against the inhabitants of their own city of origin, including their relatives. This religious violence is not unique in its kind, even if it is new at the time in the Arabian Peninsula: the "biblical" violence against idolaters (such as the episodes of Phineas in Num 25:1–13 or Elijah in 1 Kgs 18), is a model in the region during late antiquity (against pagans, Jews, deviant Christians, or Sassanid Persians).[57]

On another question, Rastoin, to illustrate the fact that the Jewish tradition is "radically orthopraxis"—that in Judaism, "faith is born of doing"—quotes Exodus 24:7: "We will do and we will listen." It is interesting to note that the Qur'an quotes this passage, but reversing the verbs, as part of a controversy where Jews and Christians are accused of not being faithful to their covenant with God (Q 5:12–14). The Qur'anic community is told: "Remember God's blessing on you and the pledge with which you were bound when you said, 'We hear and we obey.' Be mindful of God: God has full knowledge of the secrets of the heart" (Q 5:7). On this subject, we can add that compared to that of Judaism, religious law in Islam is particularly simplified. Thus, the Qur'an rejects the whole edifice of the dietary laws of Judaism, which it considers a human construction (Q 3:93–94) or a divine punishment for the children of Israel (Q 4:160). On the contrary, it insists that the law is not difficult (Q 2:185) and that God wants believers to eat good things that he has bestowed upon them (Q 2:172). In this and other areas, Muslims generally like to present Islam as "the middle way."

Other points have, of course, caught my attention, but I cannot develop them here for lack of space. Thus the question of the plurality of Judaism(s) and what makes it united. For Islam too, this question arises, and it has recently been treated in a particularly detailed, original, and fruitful way by Shahab Ahmad in *What Is Islam?*[58] This book also addresses a related issue raised by Rastoin also present in Islam, that of the preeminence of legal discussions and of the tensions that exist between different poles that, for Islam, I will characterize with Ahmad as revelation (Qur'an, tradition and law), reason (philosophy), and experience (Sufism).

With regard to the question of the relationship between revelation and tradition addressed by Marc Rastoin, I refer for Islam to my own chapter in this book. For the content of Muslim theology, especially in contemporary times, I refer to Rotraud Wielandt's excellent chapter, "Main Trends of Islamic Theological Thought from the Late Nineteenth Century to Present Times," in *The Oxford Handbook of Islamic Theology*.[59]

3

THE MODALITIES OF REVELATION IN ISLAM

Jean-Marc Balhan, SJ

THIS CHAPTER WILL highlight the foundations of reflection on revelation in Sunni Islam, analyzing how revelation is presented in its sources (Qur'an and Sunna) and how the main religious sciences (those of the Law, the Qur'an, and dialectical theology) develop an understanding of revelation. In conclusion we will present the synthesis made on this subject by Jalâl al-Dîn al-Suyûtî (d. 1505)[1] in a chapter of his textbook on Qur'anic sciences, which has become a classic, *al-Itqân fî 'ulûm al-qur'ân*.[2] We will focus here on the question of revelation's modalities more than on that of its content.

Other aspects of revelation in Islam could, of course, also have been presented here. Thus, Shiism developed its own doctrine, centered on an esoteric revelation transmitted by 'Alî (Muhammad's son-in-law and cousin) to his descendants (the twelve "imams" of Twelver Shiism). Moreover, access to God in Islam does not pass exclusively through revelation but also through reason (according to philosophers) or experience (according to Sufis). We lack space here to address these great subjects and many others, such as, for example, the more specific question of the different types of supernatural perception here on earth, such as that of the dream with the oneirocriticism that accompanies it, that of the vision of God, especially in the hereafter, or that of what a Christian could call "sacramentality" at work in various mediations of revelation. Last but not least, nowadays, in academic circles, the question dealt with here is renewed through the encounter between (a) the categories developed in the Islamic sources and thought expounded in this chapter, and (b) contemporary philosophy and human sciences.

Revelation according to the Qur'an

In the Beginning

In Islam, according to an interpretation of Q 7:172[3] that will be particularly appreciated by the Sufis, revelation begins, in a certain sense, even before creation, in pre-eternity, when God first made a covenant (*mîthâq*)[4] with human beings: "When your Lord took out the offspring from the loins of the Children of Âdam and made them bear witness about themselves, He said, 'Am I not your Lord [*alastu bi-rabbikum*]?' and they replied: 'Yes, we bear witness.' So you cannot say on the Day of Resurrection, 'We were not aware of this.'" God would have already mysteriously summoned all human beings, even before their birth, to recognize him as their only Lord. But it seems that human beings can forget this summons.

According to another Qur'anic passage (Q 30:30), at the dawn of their existence, human beings were created in such a way that they were naturally disposed to embrace true religion: "So [Prophet], as a man of pure faith [*hanîf*], stand firm and true in your devotion to the religion. This is the natural disposition [*fitra*] God instilled in humankind—there is no altering God's creation—and this is the right religion, though most people do not realize it." Some will go further in interpreting this passage; relying on the famous tradition of the Prophet, who says: "Every infant is born according to the *fitra*; then his parents make him a Jew or a Christian or a Magian," they

THE MODALITIES OF REVELATION IN ISLAM

will go so far as to say that human beings are born a Muslim but that, for reasons external to them, they change direction.

This is why, throughout the ages, in his mercy, God takes the initiative to renew his invitation. He addresses human beings by signs. These are everywhere in nature:

> In the creation of the heavens and earth; in the alternation of night and day; in the ships that sail the seas with goods for people; in the water which God sends down from the sky to give life to the earth when it has been barren, scattering all kinds of creatures over it; in the changing winds and clouds that run their appointed courses between the sky and earth: there are signs in all these for those who use their minds. (Q 2:164)

To those who are attentive and reflective, these signs reveal the goodness of creation and God's mercy, but they also reveal that what God has created, he can also "uncreate" in a flash as will be the case at the end of time, and then recreate it on the day of resurrection, prelude to the Judgment where everyone will have to answer for their actions.

These signs are also present in history, in the fate of peoples who have now disappeared: the ruins that dot the desert can testify to this. Indeed, the Qur'an tells us, before Muhammad, God had already sent prophets; they were rejected by their peoples and therefore suffered the consequences. The Qur'an here develops narratively what could be called a "prophetic pattern" arranged as follows: (1) God sends a prophet to tell a people to worship only him; (2) the prophet is rejected; (3) God annihilates the recalcitrant people. We see this pattern at work, for example, in the seven accounts of Q 26:10–191, which tell the stories of Mûsâ (Moses), Ibrâhîm (Abraham), Nûh (Noah), Lût (Lot) and the Arab prophets Hûd, Sâlih, and Shu'ayb. Muhammad's listeners are therefore invited to reflect and encouraged to make the right choice.

DIVINE REVELATION ACCORDING TO CHRISTIANITY, JUDAISM, AND ISLAM

As we have just seen, the prophets mentioned in the Qur'an are already mostly found in the biblical tradition, but there are also others from the Arab tradition. This epic begins with Âdam, the first prophet, and ends with Muhammad, the "Seal of the Prophets" (*khâtam al-nabiyyîn*: Q 33:40). To some of them, God delivers a scripture (*kitâb*): for example, the *Tawrat* (Torah) to Mûsâ (Moses), the *Zabûr* (the Psalms) to Dawûd (David), the *Injîl* (Gospel) to 'Isâ (Jesus), and finally the Qur'an to Muhammad, which confirms the previous Scriptures while prevailing over them (Q 5:48) because their meaning may have been altered.[5] Through all these signs, God invites human beings to recognize him as their only Lord and to behave accordingly.

The Qur'anic Experience

The Qur'anic revelation is the experience that the Prophet Muhammad and the first community of believers lived during late antiquity, at the beginning of the seventh century, for a little more than two decades (from the year 610, according to Muslim tradition), in the Arabian Peninsula, between the cities of Mecca and Medina.[6] It is the experience of a word that "descends" from God and is then communicated to the Prophet. He is asked to recite (*qara'a*) this word (Q 96:1–5) to those who will listen, which Muhammad does "in a clear Arabic tongue" (Q 26:195), in a form resembling that of rhymed prose (*saj'*), thus without presenting the characteristic measure of Arabic poetry alternating short and long syllables. It comes in the form of verses called "signs" (*âya*, pl. *âyât*), gathered in various "units of revelation" called "sura" (*sûra*):[7] "This is a *sûra* We have sent down and made obligatory: We have sent down clear *âyât* in it, so that you may take heed" (Q 24:1).

We can see (or rather hear) these features of the Qur'anic language, for example, in what Muslim tradition considers to be the first *âyât* revealed to Muhammad (Q 96:1–5). These are short verses whose rhyme can be clearly heard; they also present alliterations (in k, q, and l) within the verses themselves as well as repetitions between them (the verses revealed later will be progressively longer and less rhythmic) in a poetic language clearly made for memorization and recitation.

> Recite! In the name of your Lord who created:
> He created man from a clinging form.
> Recite! Your Lord is the Most Bountiful One
> who taught by [means of] the pen,
> taught man what he did not know.

> *iqra' bi-ismi rabbika alladhî khalaq*
> *khalaq al-insâna min 'alaq*
> *iqra' wa rabbuka al-akram*
> *alladhî 'allama bi-al-qalam,*
> *'allama al-insâna mâ lam ya'lam*

These verses also show that, according to the Qur'an, Muhammad receives his word from an "other," and this in a manner similar to the poets and soothsayers of his time, except that this "other" presents himself in the Qur'an in a very different way from them: it is the unique God who speaks and not a demon or some other supernatural being. This is one of the major reasons why the Qur'an will always deny being the word of a soothsayer or a poet (Q 26:192–228). It also denies being only a human work or "ancient fables" (Q 68:15). Likewise it challenges (*tahaddî*) its opponents several times to present something similar (e.g., in Q 17:88).[8]

Formally, in the text, the presence of this "other" usually manifests itself in the form of an omnipresent divine speaker speaking in the first-person plural (we), interacting with a singular "you" (the Prophet), and eliciting reactions in "them" (the listeners), to which the divine speaker often responds by asking the Prophet to say something (Say: "…"), in a polemical context. This scheme is partially found in Q 43:2–14, a passage that is also an exemplary illustration of the use of the three types of signs mentioned above (Qur'anic, historical, natural) in Qur'anic argumentation.

> By the Scripture that makes things clear, *We* have made it a Qur'an in Arabic so that you [people] may understand. It is truly exalted in the Mother of Scripture kept with *Us*, and full of wisdom. Should *We* ignore you and turn this reminder away from you because you are insolent people? *We* have sent many a prophet to earlier people and they mocked every one of them, so *We* have destroyed mightier people than [now] and their example has gone down in history. If *you* [Prophet] ask *them*, "Who created the heavens and earth?" *they* are sure to say, "They were created by the Almighty, the All Knowing." It is He who smoothed out the earth for you and traced out routes on it for you to find your way, who sends water down from the sky in due measure—*We* resurrect dead land with it, and likewise you will be resurrected from the grave—who created every kind of thing, who gave you ships and animals to ride on, so that you may remember your Lord's grace when you are seated on them and say, "Glory be to Him who has given us control over this; we could not have done it by ourselves. Truly it is to our Lord that we are returning."

As we will specify below, the Qur'an is generally presented as a "recitation" (*qur'ân*) that is gradually communicated to the Prophet from a heavenly scripture brought down by God. In doing so, the Qur'an also locates its origin upstream of the founding experiences of Judaism and Christianity which, according to it, proceed from the same source, even if it is situated downstream in history, being in a way their "last edition," in Arabic, for a new community.

With regard to its major themes, at first, in Mecca, the Qur'an invites men (who "associate" other deities with God and behave unjustly) to recognize the one God through his signs that it helps to read and interpret, and to behave accordingly. At the same time, it announces the Day of Judgment on which everyone will be judged solely according to their actions. In a second step, in Medina (i.e., *madinat al-nabî*, "the city of the Prophet"), to which the Messenger of God emigrated (*hijra*) in 622 after the opposition he encountered in his hometown, the Qur'an also invited believers to take action against the "associators" and enacted new norms to regulate worship, social relations, and the organization of this new community of believers of which Muhammad was both the legislator and the judge, as well as the leader.

The above passage also illustrates the self-referential aspect of the Qur'an, that is, the fact that it speaks of itself, especially of the way in which it descended and was communicated to the Prophet, and by him proclaimed to those who will listen. The Qur'an is therefore itself the first author of its own "theology of revelation," which we must now elucidate.[9]

The Qur'an by Itself

In the Qur'an, the notion of revelation is expressed mainly with derivatives of two verbal roots: *n-z-l* (to descend) and *w-h-y* (to communicate), as shown, for example, by the following verse: "These are the verses of the clear Scripture [*kitâb*]. We have sent it down [*n-z-l*] as an Arabic recitation [*qur'ân*]; maybe you [people] will understand. We tell you [Prophet] the best of stories in communicating [*w-h-y*] this recitation to you. Before this, you were one of the heedless" (Q 12:1–3).

As the root *n-z-l* (descend) indicates, revelation takes place first of all in a spatial context where God is above, in heaven, and humanity here on earth. From above, God "sends down" various realities such as rain (one of the many signs of nature: see Q 43:11 quoted above). Through this "sending down," God shows his benevolence and mercy toward humanity and how he intervenes in our world.

DIVINE REVELATION ACCORDING TO CHRISTIANITY, JUDAISM, AND ISLAM

He also sends down his message. Here, the Qur'an refers several times to a heavenly archetype that has several names: "Mother of Scripture" (*umm al-kitâb*, as in Q 43:4 quoted above); it is also described as a "Reminder" (*tadhkira*) said to be on "honored, exalted pure pages" (*suhuf*) written by "the hands of noble and virtuous scribes" (Q 80:13). In Q 85:21–22, it is described as "a glorious Qur'an on a Preserved Tablet" (*lawh mahfûz*). In all these situations, there is a distinction between the revealed message and its "support." However, the term most often used in the Qur'an to refer to the heavenly archetype is that of *kitâb* (Scripture, as in Q 12:1 quoted above). Often this Scripture is said to have been "sent down upon" the Prophet but also upon his listeners. However, the Prophet does not have unlimited access to all of this Scripture: potentially available, Scripture still remains out of his reach after having been "sent down"; as we shall see, Scripture will still have to be "communicated" to him, in a particular way. As for his listeners, they have access to Scripture only through the Prophet.

Some Quranic passages indicate that this Scripture was sent down at a specific time. For example, in Q 97:1–5: "We sent it down on the Night of Decree [*laylat al-qadr*]. What will explain to you what that Night of Decree is? The Night of Decree is better than a thousand months; on that night the angels and the Spirit descend again and again by the leave of their Lord upon every command; peace that night until the break of dawn." And in Q 44:2–6: "By the clear Scripture, truly We sent it down on a blessed night—We have always sent warnings—a night when every command was made distinct at Our command—We have always sent—as a mercy from your Lord who sees and knows all."

Muslim tradition will explain that Scripture was sent down during that night all at once "into the lower heaven."[10] This is not explicitly stated in the Qur'an, but while Qur'anic cosmology accepts seven heavens (see, e.g., Q 2:29), the inference is easily understandable. In any case, according to the Qur'an, even "sent down," Scripture still remains in the heavenly realm, beyond the reach of the Prophet.

THE MODALITIES OF REVELATION IN ISLAM

In a few rare verses, another type of sending down takes place, involving divine messengers such as Jibrîl (Gabriel) (Q 2:97) or "the Trustworthy Spirit" (*al-ruh al-amîn*) (Q 26:192–94, understood by the tradition to mean Jibrîl). In these passages, with God's permission, these messengers bring the Qur'an down upon the heart of the Prophet. In this case, it is no longer the archetype, Scripture, that has been sent down by God from one celestial domain to another, but the message that is brought into the earthly realm by an angelic messenger on the heart of the Prophet.

With the root *w-h-y*, we leave the space domain to enter another register: that of communication. Used in pre-Islamic poetry to designate a communication unintelligible to the outside observer (e.g., because of the passage of time or cultural difference), understood only by its recipient,[11] this root refers in the Qur'an, in almost all cases, to a communication by God to those he has chosen: the prophets.

Q 42:51 explains the three ways in which God "speaks" to his creatures: "It is not granted to any mortal that God should speak [*k-l-m*] to him except (1) through communication [*w-h-y*], or (2) from behind a veil (*hijâb*), or (3) by sending a messenger to communicate [*w-h-y*] by his command what he will: He is exalted and wise." In the first case, where God "speaks" directly, he does so by *wahy*, that is, in such a way as to be understood only by his recipient. The second case seems to refer to a visionary experience, where God appears "veiled," perhaps as in the episode of the Burning Bush with Moses, not excluding the *wahy*. It could be, for Muhammad, the experience described in Q 53:1–18, which the Muslim tradition places in the context of his ascension (*mi'râj*).[12] As for the third case, mediation by an angelic messenger, this is the preferred mode of revelation to Muhammad according to Muslim tradition. By privileging this one, the tradition probably wishes to maintain a distance between God and his creation:

> Despite there being no example of an angelic messenger communicating to the Messenger in the Qur'an through

wahy, angelic messengers do "bring down" the revelation upon the Messenger's heart (Q 2:97 and 26:193–194), and angels are said "to descend" when the celestial archetype was sent down by God (Q 97:4). It is not inconceivable that the Messenger therefore also received revelation through this mode: the angels first descend and/or bring down the revelation—likely from the celestial archetype…and then they communicate it to him.[13]

Most of the time, what is communicated by God is the recitation (*qur'ân*), but it can also be specific parts of it, for example, "the best of stories" (Q 12:3) or, more precisely, some of them, such as this or that story of prophets. It should be noted that "Scripture" (*kitâb*) is never "communicated" as such. If it is sometimes so, it is only preceded by a partitive particle: "from the Scripture" (*min al-kitâb*). A command may also be "communicated"; in this case, most of the time, it is addressed to a biblical prophet, but also sometimes to creation (to bees or to the seven heavens). There remains a mysterious verse (Q 42:52)—that follows the one that explains how God speaks to his creatures quoted above—in which what is communicated is a "spirit" (*rûh*). "Such a spirit might well imbue God's chosen elect with prophecy, and thus the ability to decipher the coded messages of *wahy*."[14]

The revelation process according to the Qur'an can therefore be summarized as follows.[15] Heavenly Scripture is sent down (*n-z-l*) by God in a single night, while remaining in the heavenly realm. It thus becomes available: for the prophets, through a "communication" of a special kind (*w-h-y*); and for humanity, by the prophets. God communicates his message from this descended Scripture (and perhaps also without passing through it). Even though in the Qur'an no angel "communicates" with the Prophet, it is mentioned that they intervene in the revelational process by sending the message down on his heart, which they can do by descending themselves from the celestial realm to the earthly realm.

THE MODALITIES OF REVELATION IN ISLAM

In addition to explaining the modalities of revelation, these two roots also have a rhetorical function:

> On the one hand, the concept of divine sending down affirms the divine origin of the revelatory message in the celestial sphere and shows that the act is predicated of God. By the late Meccan period, the act is affirmed as congruous with earlier revelations. Moreover, as the celestial event is depicted as having import for the audience of the revelation, it is also indicative of God's benevolence towards mankind by offering the potential for access to revelatory knowledge. On the other hand, the concept of divine communication is concerned with the status of the Messenger, as it attests that he is receiving revelation and is endowed with the ability to decode the communication. He is therefore divinely guided. This specific mode of receiving revelation is shared with earlier messengers, and as a result the Messenger's revelatory experience conforms to existing prophetological [*sic*] paradigms.[16]

Before concluding with a brief comparison between revelation in the Qur'an and that in the biblical tradition, let us mention a Qur'anic exception to what we have described: the revelation to Mûsâ (Moses) to which Muslim scholars will allude when studying the modality of revelation.[17] Contrary to what Q 42:51 quoted above states, but in accordance with what is said in the biblical Book of Exodus (Exod 33:10), it is said in Q 4:164, "To Mûsâ God spoke directly" (*kallama taklîman*). Then, while God "sends down" the Scripture to the Prophet, it is mentioned several times that God "gave" Mûsâ the Scripture (from the verb *âtâ*, e.g., in Q 17:2). This perhaps indicates a difference in the mode of revelation between Mûsâ and Muhammad: "while the Qur'anic Messenger had an ongoing revelation through *wahy*, which was delivered to mankind as an oral recitation drawn from a celestial scripture, *qur'ân*, Mûsâ is said to have been given a [portion] of the celestial archetype, which was manifested on earth when he received 'the tablets'" (*al-alwâh*, Q 7:145)."[18] To 'Îsâ (Jesus) is also "given" the *injîl* (gospel, Q 5:46).

These last remarks invite us to briefly compare what God "reveals" and how he does it, in the Qur'an and in the biblical tradition. In the Qur'an, to act in history God sends down "things": for example, rain, drought, his help, or, in the revelational context, Scripture or one of its forms (recitation, sura, verse…). But God himself never comes down, even if he also communicates by *wahy* with the prophets. There is an important difference here from the biblical tradition. In fact, here God acts differently in history. God rarely sends down anything. On the other hand, in the First Testament, God himself comes down (see, e.g., Gen 11:5; Exod 19:11; Ps 18:10). And according to Christian tradition, God himself, in his Son (who is also his "word"), comes down from heaven.

In fact, in the Prologue of John's Gospel we read: "The word became flesh and dwelt among us." The Nicene-Constantinople Creed (NC) (381) specifies, in a spatial context, that "the Only Begotten Son of God…true God born of true God…descended from heaven." The Creed goes on to declare: "Through the Holy Spirit he took flesh of the Virgin Mary and became man." In the Gospel of Luke, the incarnation was announced to Mary by the angel Gabriel, while a little later in the Gospel accounts, the Spirit descends on Jesus at his baptism from an open heaven. The NC will also declare that the Holy Spirit "spoke through the prophets." From all this, we can very briefly make some illuminating comparisons.

When the Qur'an speaks of a Spirit coming from God (e.g., Q 97:4; Q 26:193), Muslim tradition understands it to mean Jibrîl (Gabriel).[19] The *qur'ân*, sent down by the angel on Muhammad's heart, is "word of God." By reciting that word, the Prophet will bring the word to "birth" in the world; by hearing, memorizing, then reciting it in their turn, the listeners will enter into "communion" with the word, memorizing and reciting the word in turn. As for Muhammad, like Mary, he is "a virgin" in his own register since, the Qur'an tells us, he is *ummî* (Q 7:157–58). This word, which can be interpreted in various ways,[20] for example as "gentile" (who does not know the "Scripture"), will, however, generally be understood by Muslims to mean "unlettered" or "illiterate" (who can neither read nor write). Muhammad is therefore perfectly "virgin" of any scripture, ready to receive the *qur'ân* brought down for him by Jibrîl, as a sign that can come only from God.

From Oral to Written, from Written to Oral

The oral recitation (*qur'ân*) communicated to the Prophet and proclaimed continuously by him for twenty years will be gradually put into writing, then compiled and edited after his death in 632 in the form of the "Qur'an." The Muslim tradition presents us with this adventure of the beginnings of the writing,[21] which it concludes by saying that the text, or more precisely its consonantal *ductus* (*rasm*), was fixed during the caliphate of 'Uthmân (644–56) in what will be called the "'Uthmânic codex" (*mushaf 'Uthmân*), while the versions that differed from it were destroyed.[22] The still defective spelling (diacritical points, vowels…) will be specified only gradually beginning in the eighth century. In the end, several slightly different variants of reading (*qirâ'ât*) will be accepted, each of them based on an authority. Seven will be recognized as canonical in the tenth century,[23] and the standardization of the text in use today dates from this time.

The canonical Qur'anic codex is divided into 114 textual units called "suras" by analogy with the units of revelation mentioned in the Qur'an. With the exception of the briefest, they are each polythematic and deal with various subjects in different literary genres. In the Qur'anic corpus, they are classified by decreasing size, the first being a short prayer (*al-Fâtiha*, "the one that opens") and the last three consisting of a profession of faith, followed by two invocations to God.

In the end, the *qur'ân* (recitation) thus also became a *kitâb* ("scripture" but also "book"): the Qur'an literally became a "scripture," like its heavenly archetype and as it probably befits any revelation worthy of the name in this era of late antiquity. However, appearing phenomenologically as oral recitation, it is first "an acoustic experience" and is traditionally transmitted with authority in this form. Its proclamation in this mode throughout the ages still allows the believer today to relive the inaugural experience of revelation.

Revelation, Tradition, and the Prophet
The Sunna

At the time of the Prophet's death, the Qur'an was the sole guide of the believers. But soon new questions arose and they started to search for a new source of authority. They then began to collect the traditions of the Prophet, chosen (*mustafà*) by God to receive revelation, and his privileged interpreter. This is how the Sunna would be constituted. This was in the form of a set of hadiths, that is, stories that tell and transmit a "behavior" or a "saying" of Muhammad.[24] The hadith would soon consist of two parts: a chain of guarantors (*isnâd*), composed of an unbroken series of authoritative transmitters going back to the first witness, and a text (*matn*) that tells the story. The chain of transmitters is, of course, a guarantor of the authenticity of the story transmitted, but it is also for the believers, more or less distant from the founding event, a means of "reaching out across" beyond the spatial and temporal distances to Muhammad (in a way similar to the "apostolic succession" in the Catholic Church).

The hadiths, first transmitted in oral form, will gradually be written down and compiled into collections. Parallel with this process, a science of Hadith is developed, one of the main objectives of which will be to establish the degree of authenticity of traditions and therefore their reliability, based mainly on the criticism of their chain of transmission. Indeed, as master and model of believers, Muhammad is an ideal that many will want to imitate, sometimes even in the most trivial details. And because this ideal is to be pursued in all ages, the "invention" of new traditions in order to answer new questions (or justify various options) with reference to the prophetic model will quickly take place. This is the reason why the science of Hadith will focus mainly on the study of their authenticity.

Six collections (*kutub al-sitta*), composed in the ninth century, will finally enjoy special recognition in Sunni Islam. Those of Bukhârî (d. 870) and Muslim (d. 875), considered the most reliable, will for this reason be called *sahîh*, authentic.[25] In these collections, traditions are classified according to themes relating mainly to faith and worship, morals, and the life of the Muslim, and thus complement the Qur'an or interpret it in cases where it is silent or incomplete on certain subjects.

Revelation in the Sunna

Several books of the *Sahîh* of Bukhârî deal with the Qur'an. In the first, entitled "The Beginning of Revelation [*wahy*]," four hadiths (2–5) relate Muhammad's personal experience of revelation. The third, recounting the beginnings of this one, is particularly famous. At that time, says his wife 'Â'isha, Muhammad used to regularly take a few days of retreat at the cave of Hirâ. That's where he was when suddenly

> the angel came to him and asked him to recite. The Prophet replied, "I do not know how to recite." The Prophet added, "Then the angel caught me and pressed me so hard that I could not bear it any more. He then released me and again asked me to recite and I replied, "I do not know how to recite." Thereupon he caught me again and pressed me a second time till I could not bear it any more. He then released me and again asked me to recite but again I replied, "what shall I recite?" Thereupon he caught me for the third time and pressed me, and then

DIVINE REVELATION ACCORDING TO CHRISTIANITY, JUDAISM, AND ISLAM

released me and said, "Recite in the Name of your Lord who created"....

that is, Q 96:1–5, quoted at the beginning of this chapter. In the second hadith, Muhammad tells how revelation usually takes place. He stresses the particularly painful aspect: "Sometimes, like the ringing of a bell, this form is the hardest of all, and then this state passes off after I have grasped what he said. Sometimes the angel comes in the form of a man and talks to me and I grasp whatever he says." 'Â'isha added: "On a very cold day, I saw the revelation [*wahy*] coming down on the Prophet; as it stopped, sweat was dropping from his forehead."[26]

Muslims will want to be sure that the Qur'an they have corresponds to what God revealed to his Prophet. For this they will, of course, be able to count on the perfect knowledge that he had of it. In chapter 7 of book 66 of the *Sahîh* entitled "The Virtues of the Qur'an," we can indeed read that, shortly before his death, he confided to his daughter Fâtima: "Jibrîl [Gabriel] used to check my knowledge of the Qur'an once in a year, but this year he did it twice. I do not think but that my death is approaching."[27]

However, in this context, Muslims will also have to account for a relative diversity in the recitation of certain suras. On this subject, a hadith will make much ink flow: "The Qur'an was sent down according to seven *harf*." Tradition will wonder what is the precise meaning of the word *harf*, which could be translated as "variant."[28] Bukhârî, in the same book of his Sahîh, tells us the following episode, attested by Ibn 'Abbâs, according to which the Messenger of God says: "Jibrîl recited to me according to a *harf*. Then I requested him and went on asking him to continue, and he added, till he finished with seven *harf*." According to this hadith, the origin of the variants is therefore at the very source of the revelation, in the request of the Prophet. This hadith is followed by another on the same subject, which explains one of the possible reasons why the Prophet asked for several versions of the recitation. He tells us that 'Umar [one of the Companions of the Prophet and future caliph] heard someone reciting a sura according to a *harf* that he had never heard from the Messenger of God. 'Umar therefore took him close to himself, and the Prophet asked them both to recite this sura. Although their recitations were different, the Prophet said to each of them, "It was sent down in this way." Then he added: "This Qur'an has been sent down according to seven *harf*. So, recite of it whichever is easier for you."[29] It would therefore have been to enable everyone to recite the Qur'an easily that it would have been sent down according to several *harf*.

Finally, still in this same book, chapter 3 tells us the story of "the collection of the Qur'an": first by Zayd ibn Thâbit, Muhammad's secretary, at the request of the first caliph, Abû Bakr. Later, and in another hadith, a Companion of the Prophet, seeing that the Iraqis and Syrians differed in their way of reciting the Qur'an, said to 'Uthmân, the third caliph: "O chief of the believers! Save this nation before they differ about the Scripture as Jews and Christians did before." 'Uthmân then asked four people to copy and possibly correct Zayd's manuscript.[30] He then had a copy sent to each province and ordered the destruction of all other Qur'anic material.

The Sunna as Revelation

The Sunna will be used, with the Qur'an, as the basis for reflection in the various religious sciences, especially in the study of the Law (*fiqh*), but also in exegesis (*tafsîr*), theology (*'ilm al-kalâm*), and mysticism (*tasawwuf*).

Initially, not all scholars agreed among themselves on the Sunna's importance. It was the jurist Shâfi'î (d. 820) who finally allowed the traditionalists' camps to win the battle. In his *Risâla*, his treatise on the foundations of Islamic law (*usûl al-fiqh*), he established that "God has imposed on believers the obligation to conform to His Revelation and the traditions of His Messenger." He does this by interpreting a series of Qur'anic verses mentioning that God teaches his messengers "scripture and wisdom [*hikma*]" (e.g., in Q 62:2) as meaning that God teaches the Qur'an and the Sunna, for "Wisdom is the Sunna of God's Messenger," he claims. "The Sunna of God's Messenger explains the meanings willed by God. They indicate the particular meaning or general meaning of divine discourse. Furthermore, God linked Wisdom to the Sunna and His Book by mentioning it immediately after them. He has not conferred this [privilege] on any of his creatures other than on his Messenger."[31]

Subsequently, the reflection on the Sunna, now compiled in canonical collections, will lead to its status being clarified in relation to the Qur'an. The word of God (*kalâm Allah*) will then be conceived as composed of two parts: a stylish speech, called to be recited publicly and literally, the Qur'an, and a speech not intended for public recitation, uttered by the Prophet not according to the letter but according to the meaning, the Sunna. We find this, for example, already in Ghazâlî (d. 1111),[32] and then Suyûtî (d. 1505) in his treatise on Qur'anic sciences.[33] The Sunna has thus also become equally the word of God, even if it is not verbatim.[34]

Some hadiths, called "holy" (*qudsî*), also have a special status because, in these, the Prophet cites God as their author. However, not being literally the word of God, they do not have the same status as the Qur'an. Regarding their communication to the Prophet, Muslim tradition thinks that Jibrîl is not necessarily the intermediary, but that Muhammad may have received them in dreams, by inspiration (*ilhâm*), or during a heavenly ascension (*mi'râj*) that we will discuss shortly.

The Sîra of the Prophet and Devotion to His Person

In addition to the thematic collections of hadith mentioned above, the *Sîra* of the Prophet, his biography, is also elaborated, welcoming hadiths telling episodes of his life. It takes its first form under the pen of Ibn Ishâq (d. 767), which has come down to us in a form reworked by Ibn Hishâm (d. 833). They and their successors collected everything that could be found about Muhammad for the sake of integrity and put it in narrative form. Later, in the Middle Ages, the traditionalists sorted it out, in a critical spirit but also so that the *Sîra* was more usable by the believers, in their faith or their moral life.

The Prophet who, in the Qur'an, was first and foremost a human being, not devoid of weaknesses, and who owed his special status to his election by God and therefore to the Qur'an which, on his side, he transmitted, gradually saw his status rise and supernatural abilities unfold over time.[35] In this context, a reflection on his impeccability (*'isma*) also took place: opinions differed according to the theological schools,[36] but it was resolutely affirmed in Shiism. "Veneration of the Prophet, the interest in even the smallest details of his behavior and personal life grew in the same measure as the Muslims were distanced from him in time. They wanted to know ever more about his personality, his looks and his words in order to be sure that they were following him correctly."[37] Thus were born two new literary genres: the *dalâ'il al-nubuwwa* (proofs of prophetic stature) detailing his miracles and that of the *shamâ'il* (virtues) of the Prophet exposing his qualities and beauty both physical and spiritual. Muhammad, who became master and model, wonderworker, and even, finally, intercessor on the Day of Judgment, became more and more over the centuries, an object of love and devotion for believers, as evidenced by the famous work of Qâdî 'Iyâd (d. 1149), *Kitâb al-Shifâ*.[38]

In this spirit, famous poems (*na't*) are composed on the Prophet even if, God having already praised the Prophet in the Qur'an, the authors know themselves unable to emulate their Lord. Of all these poems recited and sung in the Muslim world, until today, on the occasion of the great feasts of the Prophet, the most famous is *Qasîdat al-Burda* (Mantle Ode) of Busîrî (d. ca. 1294–97), which is also a true summary of medieval "prophetology."

Mysterious events in the Qur'an concerning the privileged relationship between the Prophet and God will know many developments in the Muslim tradition, as also in theology, mysticism, literature and poetry, art, and worship: the night journey (*isrâ'*) of Muhammad "from the sacred place of worship to the furthest place of worship" (Q 17:1) followed by his ascension (*mi'râj*) (Q 81:19–25; Q 53:1–18). Tradition will gradually specify that this nocturnal journey is made on a heavenly mount called Burâq, to the Temple Mount in Jerusalem, where he will meet Ibrâhîm (Abraham), Mûsâ (Moses), 'Îsâ (Jesus), and other prophets, before leading a prayer in their company; he will then climb the seven heavens, accompanied by the angel Gabriel. During his ascension, he will meet prophets of old, before speaking with God himself by asking him, under the advice of Mûsâ, to reduce the number of daily canonical prayers imposed on the believer from fifty to five. In this episode, it is no longer a scripture that is "sent down" and then communicated to the Messenger, but the Prophet who is "sent up" to finally converse with God. If theologians will wonder whether these events took place when the Prophet was awake or sleeping, with his body or with his mind, to the Sufis these events will offer a paradigm for their own mystical journey, and to the community of believers a vision to ignite their imagination, allowing them to accompany their Prophet on his initiatory journey.

Muhammad, Alpha and Omega of Creation

We have begun this chapter on revelation in Islam by mentioning its first occurrence in pre-eternity, with the *mîthâq*. According to mystics, the story of Muhammad also begins in pre-eternity, in a luminous form, the light of Muhammad (*nûr Muhammad*). This will also be the case in Shiite Islam, with other consequences.

Already in the Qur'an, God calls the Prophet "a light-giving lamp" (*sirâj munîr*) (Q 33:46); then in the *Sîra* of Ibn Hishâm, an allusion is also made to a light that was carried by his father before the conception of Muhammad and that disappeared afterward, to reappear at his nativity. His mother, in giving birth, "noticed that a light sprang from her." This idea of the "light of Muhammad" will spread widely in Islamic literature.

The Iraqi mystic Sahl al-Tustarî (d. 896) is one of the first authors to mention the preexistence of this "light of Muhammad." It is found in his Qur'anic commentary, mainly in his commentary on verse Q 7:172 referring to the primordial covenant (*mîthâq*), quoted at the beginning of this chapter ("When your Lord took out the offspring from the loins of the Children of Âdam and made them bear witness about themselves..."). In his commentary, he uses the vocabulary of a famous parable of the Qur'an, the "Verse of Light" (Q 24:35), in which the "lamp" contained therein is interpreted by him as the symbol of the Prophet:

> God is the Light of the heavens and earth. His Light is like this: there is a niche, and in it a lamp, the lamp inside a glass, a glass like a glittering star, fuelled from a blessed olive tree from neither east nor west, whose oil almost gives light even when no fire touches it—light upon light—God guides whoever He will to his Light; God draws such parables for people; God has full knowledge of everything. (Q 24:35)

Tustarî therefore comments Q 7:172:

> The progeny comprise three [parts], a first, second and third: *The first is Muḥammad,* for when God, Exalted is He, wanted to create Muḥammad, He made appear a light from His light, and when it reached the veil of divine majesty it prostrated before God, and from that prostration God created an immense crystal-like column of light, that was inwardly and outwardly translucent and within it was the essence of Muḥammad. Then it stood in service before the Lord of the Worlds for a million years with the essential characteristics of faith.... *The second*

> *among the progeny is Adam.* God created him from the light of Muḥammad. And He created Muḥammad, that is, his body, from the clay of Adam. *The third is the progeny of Adam.* God, Mighty and Majestic is He, created the seekers [of God] from the light of Adam, and He created the [divinely]-sought from the light of Muḥammad. Thus, the generality among people live under the mercy of the people of proximity and the people of proximity live under the mercy of the one brought near [i.e., the Prophet].[39]

These ideas will be taken up and developed by many other mystics (Mansûr al-Hallâj, Farîd al-Dîn 'Attâr, Jalâl al-Dîn Rûmî, Yunus Emre…); systematized by Ibn 'Arabî (d. 1240), they will then continue to spread:

> In Sufism after Ibn 'Arabî, the preexistent essence of the Prophet, called *al-haqîqa al-muhammadiyya*, is considered to be the fountainhead of all prophetic activity. For this *haqîqa muhammadiyya*—a term often translated "archetypal Muhammad"—manifests itself first in Adam, then in all the other prophets until it finds its full expression once more in the historical Muhammad, who thus becomes, as it were, the Alpha and Omega of creation. Muhammad the Prophet is the all-comprehensive and perfect manifestation of the primordial light, and with him the cycle of manifestation is completed, for he is the Seal of the Prophets.[40]

From another point of view, no longer that of the origin but that of the end, Muhammad will also become the Perfect Man (*insân kâmil*), in view of whom man has been created, the completion, fulfilment, and goal of all human life—according to Ibn 'Arabî and his successors, in particular 'Abd al-Karîm al-Jîlî (d. 1408) who wrote a key text on this topic.[41]

Revelation and Islamic Religious Sciences
Revelation and Islamic Law

The science of Islamic law, Islamic jurisprudence (*fiqh*), is a major discipline in Sunni Islam. How does the Qur'anic revelation have a "legal" dimension? If we look at the text, we will first notice that the number of normative verses is quite small. In this area, the Meccan suras are generally limited to inviting people to practice justice and to show solidarity with the poor, without requiring divine instructions as to the precise content of what is required or as to knowing what precisely justice is. The strictly normative verses are mostly found in the Medinan suras, in connection with Muhammad's new function as arbiter[42] of the new community being formed, but also in a context in which Muhammad is likewise in contact with Jewish communities, which have a religious law (*halakha*).

In this new context, the Prophet makes judgments in the name of God, but without constructing precise political frameworks. In general, the Qur'an invites human beings to obey not only God, but also his Messenger (which will later provide an argument for integrating the Prophet's tradition into the sources of *fiqh*) and those who hold authority (Q 4:59). They must judge fairly; the Muslim community, on the other hand, must "call for what is good, urge what is right, and forbid what is wrong" (Q 3:104). But the Medinan revelations also contain more precise obligations relating to rite, morality, and social organization.

One may wonder why the Qur'an establishes a religious law, since the practical problems faced by the first community could be solved by Muhammad outside of a revelation. The presence of a religious law is therefore not a mere accident of history, but a properly theological choice. This choice is well explained in Q 5:44–50, which asks Muhammad to *judge according to what God has revealed*, as he had already previously asked the Jews and those who follow the Gospel.

> We sent down the Torah with guidance and light; and the prophets, who had submitted to God, judged according to it for the Jews. So did the rabbis and the scholars in accordance with that part of God's Scripture which they were entrusted to preserve, and to which they were witnesses. So [rabbis and scholars] do not fear people, fear Me; do not barter away My messages for a small price; those who do not judge according to what God has sent down are rejecting [God's teachings].....
>
> We sent Jesus, son of Mary, in their footsteps, to confirm what was before him, from the Torah: We gave him the Gospel with guidance, light, and confirmation of what was before him, from the Torah—a guide and lesson for those who take heed of God. So let the followers of the Gospel judge according to what God has sent down in it. Those who do not judge according to what God has sent down are lawbreakers.
>
> We sent down to you [Muhammad] the Scripture with the truth, confirming what was before it from the Scripture, and with final authority over them: so judge between them according to what God has sent down. Do not follow their whims, which deviate from the truth that has come to you. We have assigned a law and a path to each of you....

The Medinan law thus provided the new Muslim community with a new religious law. In addition to local customs, Jewish law, Christian law (the *Didascalia Apostolorum*), and perhaps also imperial Roman law seem to have been dialogue partners of the Qur'an.[43]

While one can speak of the institution of norms in the Qur'an, one cannot speak of a legal system. It was only later that these norms would be used as a source, or rather as an endorsement, of a legal doctrine, the *fiqh*, which appeared at the beginning of the eighth century and also integrated other legal cultures of its environment. Little by little, it covered all aspects of religious, civil, and political life. We will therefore find laws regulating ritual and religious observances (*'ibâdât*) and others regulating the family, inheritance, property, and contracts, that is to say, social life (*mu'âmalât*), as well as criminal, constitutional, and war law.

The birth of this discipline is accompanied by that of a science of its foundations (*usûl al-fiqh*), which, little by little, articulates its sources and rationalizes the methodology.[44] Its major founder was Shâfi'î, with his *Risâla*, which we have previously met, when we explained how this work contributed to enhancing the status of the Sunna. The *Risâla* recognizes four foundations for the *fiqh*: the Qur'an, the Sunna, the consensus of the community (*ijmâ'*), and analogical reasoning (*qiyâs*), articulated differently according to the different legal schools (*madhhab*) of Sunni Islam that emerged during the first centuries of Islam (*Mâlikî, Hanafî, Shâfi'î,* and *Hanbalî*). Gradually, these recognized each other and were recognized as valid interpretations of the religious law of Islam.

From the end of the tenth century, a consensus gradually spread to restrict the use of independent legal reasoning to scholars of the past and therefore require the insertion of jurists in one of these schools. Over time, new issues arose in relation to new developments; legal opinions (*fatwa*) are then issued by legal consultants (*muftî*) who use established juridical sciences to answer these new questions as best as possible. If these legal opinions are recognized by the common opinion of scholars, they are integrated into the legal corpus of their school.

However, when one moves from (a) the theory of *fiqh* conceived by scholars to (b) the practice of judges (*qâdî*), the formal rules of Islamic law do not always show themselves capable of resolving concrete questions. This is why, little by little, from the end of the eighth century, the administration of most of the criminal justice system was taken over by the police and a significant part of the administration of civil justice escaped from the *qâdî*, their competence gradually being limited to the law of the family, inheritance, and foundations. Thus, in most Muslim countries there has been a dual administration of justice.

Revelation and Sciences of the Qur'an

Alongside the previous religious sciences, those of the Qur'an (*'ulûm al-Qur'ân*) were established. Among these we find those that study the modalities of the revelation of the Qur'an or the progressive establishment of the canonical text. The science of the "occasional causes of descent" (*asbâb al-nuzûl*) studies the circumstances in which a verse or group of verses was "brought down" on the Prophet; this science is the object of careful studies, the basic material of which is the tradition of the Prophet, especially the *Sîra*. For the Muslim community, this science was important to historicize revelation; it remains so for the modern exegete who raises the question of the purposes of revelation or for the jurist who asks the question of the goals (*maqâsid*) of the divine law.

Another science, that of "the abrogating and the abrogated" (*al-nâsikh wa al-mansûkh*), makes it possible to discern an evolution in the Qur'anic revelation that took place for twenty years. It is based on Q 2:106, which says: "Any verse [*âya*] We cause to be superseded or forgotten, We replace with something better or similar. Do you [Prophet] not know that God has power over everything?" The question debated by scholars is whether the abrogated verses still appear in the final version of the Qur'an. In the latter case, it is then up to the exegete to situate the verses chronologically in relation to one another with the help of the science of "occasional causes of the descent." This question is important for the "doctors of the Law" who have to determine the definitive standard established by the divine Lawgiver. Modernist authors will also use this theory of abrogation to legitimize an evolutionary exegesis that would conceive the logical consequences of certain legal provisions of the Qur'an, given the new realities facing the Muslim community.[45]

We can also mention the sciences that study the style of the Qur'an, its various literary genres (stories, oaths, norms, and so forth) and its rhetoric: the study of the language of the Qur'an, gradually considered perfect, will be at the source of the development of Arabic grammar; it will also intervene, as we shall soon see, in the establishment of the doctrine of inimitability (*i'jâz*) of the Qur'an, proof par excellence of its divine origin and therefore of Muhammad's prophecy.

The science of the Qur'an par excellence, exegesis (*tafsîr*), will use these disciplines and other Islamic religious sciences. After the Prophet himself some of his Companions are recognized as the first interpreters of the revelation. Among these, Ibn 'Abbâs (d. 688), cousin of the Prophet, is recognized by tradition as the first author of a Qur'anic commentary, and his *Tafsîr* will be the main reference work of the Muslim exegetes who will follow. The methodology of the first commentaries is traditional: it relies on chains of transmitters going back to the Prophet, his Companions, or their successors, and tries to restore the primitive tradition of revelation. This traditional interpretation will culminate in Tabarî's commentary (d. 923). After him, over the centuries, came many works commenting on and interpreting Qur'anic verses from various perspectives (linguistic, legal, theological, mystical…) and different methodological options (such as privileging the letter or the spirit of the text). We have seen above an example of a mystical commentary in Tustarî's interpretation of Q 7:172 in his *Tafsîr*.

If the Qur'an is a text read, studied, and commented on as the book in which "God put the science of all things," it is also recited orally throughout the Muslim world by following one of the seven readings mentioned above, according to precise rules set forth in another Qur'anic science called *tajwîd*. Most Muslims do not know Arabic, but they can recite in this language at least the verses used

DIVINE REVELATION ACCORDING TO CHRISTIANITY, JUDAISM, AND ISLAM

for the canonical ritual prayer (*salât*). Even today, the basic teaching in Islam is that of rote learning of the Qur'an in Arabic, and those who manage to memorize it in its entirety receive the envied title of *hâfiz*. For believers, listening to the recitation of the Qur'an has an almost "sacramental" character that makes them experience anew the original revelation.

Several authors of *Tafsîr* introduce the sciences of the Qur'an at the beginning of their work, but works will also be exclusively devoted to them. The most famous of these is "Excellence in the Sciences of the Qur'an" (*al-Itqân fî 'ulûm al-qur'an*) by Jalâl al-Dîn al-Suyûtî (d. 1505), a synthesis of those who preceded him to which the author also adds his own reflections. Regularly taken up by his successors, it remained a reference work in the following centuries. In terms of method, Suyûtî's interest is primarily in the Hadith (which he taught), but also in law, grammar, and rhetoric. He had little interest in dialectical theology (*'ilm al-kalâm*) and none at all in the "sciences of the ancients" (philosophy, logic, mathematics, and medicine).

The eighty chapters of varying size that compose this work can be grouped into nine parts that we could entitle: "Where, When, and How the Qur'an Descended" (1–16); "The Qur'an Edition" (17–19); "The Transmission of the Qur'an" (20–27); "The Recitation of the Qur'an" (28–35); "The Linguistic Aspect of the Qur'an" (36–42); "The Normative Aspect of the Qur'an" (43–50); "The Rhetoric and Inimitability of the Qur'an" (51–64); "Miscellaneous" (65–76); "The Exegesis of the Qur'an and Those Who Practice It" (77–80).

The sixteenth chapter is devoted to studying the modality of revelation and constitutes a synthesis of the Muslim tradition. We will expound on this subject by way of conclusion. But before that, we still need to look at one last religious science, dialectical theology, which, by describing the Qur'an as eternal and then inimitable, will guide its interpretation and the faith of Muslims for centuries, until today.

Revelation and Dialectical Theology

Dialectical theology (*'ilm al-kalâm*) has its origin in developments internal to Islam but also in its encounter with other traditions. First apologetic and then more "exploratory," it is based on the same four pillars as *fiqh*. One of its classic definitions is that of Ibn Khaldûn (d. 1406): "This is a science that involves arguing with logical proofs defending the articles of faith and refuting innovators who deviate in their dogmas from the early Muslims (*salaf*) and Muslim orthodoxy (*sunna*). The real core of the articles of faith is the oneness of God (*tawhîd*)."[46] This discipline gave rise to different currents: (1) the *Mu'tazilî*, rationalists attached to the Unity and Justice of God; (2) the *Hanbalî*, literalist traditionalists hostile to the excessive use of reason; (3) the *Ash'arî*, proposing a middle way that will become the majority; and (4) the *Mâturîdî*, also proposing a middle way that was more rationalist. These last two currents will come closer over the centuries.

On the subject of the modalities of revelation that concerns us here, the first question addressed by this discipline is that of the status of the attributes of God, in particular that of his word (*kalâm*). The second question is that of Muhammad's prophecy (*nubuwwa*), whose proof par excellence is the miracle of the inimitability of the Qur'an (*i'jâz*), attesting to its divine origin, which it will be necessary to specify.[47]

THE QUR'AN: NON-CREATED, UNCREATED, ETERNAL

Among the great questions that dialectical theology deals with on the theme of revelation, the first is that of the status of God's attributes. About his word, the big question is that of knowing whether it is created (position of the *Mu'tazilî*) or uncreated (the other schools, starting with the *Hanbalî*). This question will be politically marked by the "inquisition" (*mihna*) launched in 833 by the caliph al-Ma'mûn against those who refused to profess the *Mu'tazilî* position of the "Qur'an created." This position was vigorously opposed

DIVINE REVELATION ACCORDING TO CHRISTIANITY, JUDAISM, AND ISLAM

by Ibn Hanbal and his traditionalist followers. They were finally able to claim victory in 848, when another caliph, al-Mutawakkil, put an end to the *mihna*. This inquisition, which lasted fifteen years, thus turned against Mu'tazilism. Condemned as heresy, it would gradually disappear from the landscape in the Sunni Muslim world. It was not until the end of the nineteenth century that various modernist thinkers revived this school.

The question of the created/non-created Qur'an arose nearly a century before the *mihna*[48] with al-Jahm b. Safwân (d. 745) and his followers, who denied that God could "speak." According to their definition, speech is a human attribute that requires organs. So every word of God, including the Qur'an, is created by God: he creates a sound and makes it heard. This position is therefore initially an attack on the anthropomorphic and personal representation of God that was prevalent among traditionalists. On the contrary, they insisted that God speaks, that he really spoke to Moses, and that the Qur'an is not created (*laysa bi-makhlûq*) but spoken by God, without affirming, however, that it is "uncreated" (*ghayr makhlûq*).

With the *mihna*, the notion of "createdness of the Qur'an" changes meaning and is understood as implying the temporality of the Qur'an, while that of its "non-createdness" gives rise to the new notion of "uncreated Qur'an," implying that it is "eternal" (*qadîm*). This happens during the debate with the *Mu'tazilî*.

Indeed, they do not deny that God can speak or that the Qur'an is really the word of God, for they define the word other than al-Jahm b. Safwân, namely, as a set of letters and sounds. But they were vigorously opposed to anything that was coeternal with God:

> They denied any independent existence to the essential attributes in God, and strictly maintained the temporality of all attributes referring to his acts. They held, moreover, that the acts of God cannot subsist in his unchangeable essence, but must be created elsewhere. Since in affirming that the Koran is created they were chiefly concerned with

its temporality, they accuse those denying its creation of asserting its eternity and of destroying God's unity by the admission of something co-eternal with him....There the traditionalists are not charged with anthropomorphism and ascribing organs of speech to God. They are polemically accused of putting God and the Koran on an equal level....They are thus like the Christians, who claim that Jesus was not created because he is the word of God. This was a favorite argument of the Mu'tazila.[49]

To this, Ibn Hanbal will answer that (1) to give a temporal origin to the word of God would mean that there was a time when God did not speak; (2) since the Qur'an is part of the knowledge of God, the doctrine of creation of the Qur'an implies that God was originally ignorant; (3) Jesus is not the word of God, Q 4:171 meaning that he is created by it. "The traditionalist denial that the Koran was created, rather than spoken, by God thus was turned into a positive thesis, that of the eternity of the Koran."[50] The Qur'an, which had become "the uncreated word of God," will then be qualified as eternal (*qadîm*) by theologians.

From this new position, which becomes that of "orthodoxy" in Sunni Islam on the basis of several arguments, the various schools address the problem of the relationship between the eternity of the word of God and its manifestations in time. For Ash'arî (d. 936), "the divine word, like every word, is an entity [*ma'nâ*] inherent in the one who speaks; it is in itself neither letter nor sound."[51] These are only the expression of the entity "speech." In the case of the Qur'an, the words that constituted it are therefore only the manifestation of the divine word: it alone is eternal, they are created. The same applies when it comes to reciting the Qur'an, writing it down or memorizing it. While the Hanbalî see in the words themselves the eternal word of God, Ash'arî distinguishes between what is recited, which is eternal, and its recitation, which is created. This distinction led his successors (al-Juwaynî, d. 1085, and his pupil al-Ghazâlî, d. 1111) to differentiate *kalâm nafsî* (internal word) and *kalâm lafzî* (word expressed by words, in a language). Thus for Ghazâlî:

> the attribute of the Word, subsisting in the divine Essence, is first and foremost this internal Word in God, which is eternal and uncreated, without future or past, without multiplication or division. It is in no way impossible that God makes it manifest ad extra by created sounds and letters. It is essentially in this that prophetic revelation resides. Contrary to the belief of the Mu'tazilites, it is not a matter of words created in certain bodies. It is indeed God who speaks, but through sounds and letters belonging to the world of creation which manifest and express His single and immutable Word.[52]

This position will become the majority in Sunni Muslim theology, even though in the Muslim world the *Hanbalî* position, which sees in the words themselves the eternal word of God, is still held.

THE MIRACLE OF THE INIMITABILITY OF THE QUR'AN

The second question studied by dialectical theology in connection with revelation is that of prophecy (*nubuwwa*) in general, that of Muhammad in particular, whose proof par excellence is the miracle of inimitability (*i'jâz*) of the Qur'an.

Derived from the root '-*j-z*, *i'jâz* more precisely means "rendering powerless, incapable" (of producing the like of it). The Qur'anic starting point is the challenge (*tahaddî*) addressed by the Qur'an to its opponents[53] to produce "something" similar, while they accused the Prophet of being himself the author of what he recited to them (in the Qur'an, there is no trace of answers to this challenge). However, the doctrinal elaboration of this "inimitability" of the Qur'an will not begin to take shape until later.

It is indeed from the ninth century that it becomes inappropriate to find imperfections in the Qur'an, and from the tenth century that one begins to find the classical works on *i'jâz al-qur'ân*. Several historical reasons may explain the origin of the emergence of this doctrine at this time.[54] First of all, it can be noted that from the ninth century, in the context of internal debates in Islam, Muslim scholars elaborate a reflection on the definition of what is a "miracle" (*mu'jiza*) in general. Derived from the same root as the word *i'jâz*, this new word—which was present neither in the Qur'an nor in the *Sîra*, where one speaks rather of sign (*âya*) or proof (*burhân*)—will quickly take on the following technical meaning: "a thing deviating from the usual course of things, appearing at the hands of him who pretends to be a prophet, as a challenge to those who deny this, of such a nature that it makes it impossible for them to produce the like of it. It is God's testimony to the sincerity of His apostles."[55]

The ninth century was also the beginning of the controversies in the Arabic language with the Christians. The miracles of Christ and his disciples play an important role in Christian apologetics as proof of the truth of Christianity. Indeed, the doctrine of the *i'jâz* can be seen as an equivalent: a miracle that authenticates Muhammad's prophetic mission while defining its specificity. In this line, Al-Jâhiz (d. 869) thus proposes an explanatory model that will be taken up by his successors:

> God granted to each prophet...the gift that his people would value most highly. In Egypt, where magic was highly regarded, Moses outmatched the arts of Pharaoh's sorcerers by turning his staff into a snake, and was thus confirmed as a prophet. In a time when the healing arts were particularly valued, Jesus' raising the dead was the miracle that authenticated him. Muhammad is the prophet of a nation that prided itself on poets above all else, therefore his sign had to be a miracle of words.[56]

DIVINE REVELATION ACCORDING TO CHRISTIANITY, JUDAISM, AND ISLAM

In the model of Jâhiz, we see at work the first of the four elements of the rereading of history[57] that are at the foundation of the doctrine of the *i'jâz*, namely: (1) the Arabs are a nation of poets, which is why the miraculous character of the Qur'an lies in this register. Then come (2) Muhammad was illiterate and therefore could never have produced such a marvel by himself, either in substance or in form; (3) several people, including the most famous poets of their time, have tried to meet the Qur'anic challenge, but without success;[58] (4) while, on the contrary, the Qur'an amazes and fascinates all those who, over the generations, approach it. From this last point of view, the inimitability of the Qur'an is also regarded by the Muslim community as a lasting miracle that will last until the end of the world, while the miracles of the other prophets were limited to their time, subsisting only by the accounts that describe them.

Many authors have embarked on the study of *i'jâz*.[59] The most famous are, first of all, the Ash'arite judge (*qâdî*) and theologian Abû Bakr al-Bâqillânî (d. 1013), who in his *I'jâz al-Qur'ân* establishes the foundations and proofs of the Qur'anic miracle, recapitulating his predecessors and adding his own arguments; it will be taken up by many of his successors. Later, the grammarian and rhetorician 'Abd al-Qâhir al-Jurjânî (d. 1078), in his *Dalâ'il al-i'jâz*, focused exclusively on the poetic structure of the Qur'an and developed in his work "a comprehensive theory on the nature of language, meaning, the imagination and poetic imagery."[60]

According to all these authors, what is the miraculous character of the Qur'an? Does it reside in the Qur'an or outside of it? This last theory, proposed for the first time by the *mu'tazilî* Nazzâm (d. ca. 845) and then by some others belonging to this school, affirms that the miracle is not found in the Qur'an itself but in interventions of God, who diverts (*sarf*) humans from imitating him, taking away their power and motivation. This theory will be hardly retained thereafter, except by a few authors, as an auxiliary doctrine.

But then, if its miraculous character lies in the Qur'an itself, where exactly? Some authors say that its inimitability can be perceived but not described; but this solution, which is not one, does not satisfy the most rigorous of them. Does its miraculous character then lie in its content, that is, in the information it contains, for example, about future events that had not yet taken place at the time of its proclamation, or about peoples of past centuries? If this explanation was retained as one of the components of the *i'jâz*, it was not accepted as its main reason because other revealed books also have these characteristics.

Soon, most opinions clustered around stylistics and eloquence as the seat of the miracle. Bâqillânî presents the Qur'an style as unique, by nature "incomparable," while Jurjânî explains in detail its poetic structure:[61]

> the argument mainly revolves around the inevitable trinity of semantics: words [*lafz*], meanings [*ma'nâ*] and their structure/construction [*nazm*]. It is on *nazm* that the claim of a stylistic *i'jâz* will finally be staked, *nazm* standing for the relation between words in synergy with the intended meaning. Thus the Qur'an's resplendent eloquence resides in the manner in which words have been perfectly joined to each other, rendering meaning with such flawless accuracy that no word could be conceivably exchanged for another without destroying the seamless verbal fabric.[62]

Conclusion: A Classic Summary—the Revelation of the Qur'an according to Suyûtî

To conclude this presentation of the modalities of revelation in Sunni Islam, we now expound the synthesis made by Suyûtî in the sixteenth chapter of his *Itqân*, entitled precisely: "The modality of its descent [*fî kayfiyyati inzâlihî*]"[63]: he perfectly summarizes what the Muslim tradition says on this subject and which we have detailed in the previous pages.

DIVINE REVELATION ACCORDING TO CHRISTIANITY, JUDAISM, AND ISLAM

This chapter is divided into three questions. The first deals with the "spatio-temporal dimensions" of this "descent of the Qur'an" (in a cosmology with seven heavens). Muslim scholars have tried to articulate two facts: the Qur'an was sent down at a specific time, during the month of Ramadan, during the Night of the Decree (*laylat al-qadr*), says the text (Q 2:185; Q 97:1); it was also sent down "gradually," "in fragmented form," for twenty years, in different months in response to the "occasional causes of the descent." Suyûtî reports how scholars tried to hold these two propositions together and takes a position. His conclusion is that the Qur'an descended "all at once" to the lower Heaven on the Night of the Decree, and from there it descended "gradually" on the Prophet for about twenty years. God sent it down "all at once," he says, to emphasize his importance and to treat Mûsâ (who received revelation "once" in the tablets of the Law) and Muhammad equally. He sent it down "gradually" to encourage Muhammad and to allow him to learn it by heart (because the Prophet was illiterate), but also to respond adequately to circumstances and because it was composed of "the abrogating and the abrogated" (otherwise it would present contradictions).

The second question relates more precisely to the modality of the sending down (*inzâl*) of the Qur'an and its communication (*wahy*) to the Prophet. According to one author, *inzâl* can mean "manifesting" the recitation or sending Jibrîl down with the recitation; and in order for communication between Muhammad and him to take place, it is necessary either that the Prophet be clothed in the angelic form or that the angel be clothed in the human form, Suyûtî preferring the second option.

Another author provides more precision: *inzâl* would mean "to establish definitively," an expression understood differently according to the theological school to which one belonged. For the *Ash'arî*, who say that the Qur'an is "an entity residing in the essence of God," to "send it down" is for God to bring into existence the words and letters indicating this entity and to "establish it definitively" in the Preserved Table. For the *Hanbalî*, on the other hand, who say that the

Qur'an consists in the words, "to send down" is for God to "establish them definitively" in the Preserved Table. In both cases, *inzâl* can also be subsequently applied to the "establishment" of the Qur'an in the Lower Heaven. In the second stage of the descent, when it comes to sending a scripture down on a messenger, the word *inzâl* signifies an angel "descending" with Scripture to deliver it to the messenger after having learned it either from God or from the Preserved Table.

Suyûtî then looks at the content of what descended on the Prophet. There are three opinions, he tells us: Jibrîl came down with the letter and meaning of this revelation, or only with the meaning, and it is then either the Prophet or Jibrîl who expresses them in Arabic. As we have already mentioned above, Suyûtî then endorses the opinion of Juwaynî for whom the revelation took place in two different modalities, according to the meaning and according to the letter, his own interpretation being that the part revealed according to the meaning is the Sunna, and the part revealed according to the letter is the Qur'an. He then concludes his argument by justifying this differentiation in the revelation process. Some of it was revealed literally, he says, for four reasons: for the purposes of worship; to make it a miracle, an inimitable marvel; because there is a perfect balance between the letter and the meaning that refer to each other; and finally, to protect the community against change and falsification. On the other hand, some of it was revealed according to meaning to lighten the burden of the community.

Suyûtî then concludes this second question by telling how the communication (*wahy*) to the Prophet took place. He distinguishes five modalities: the angel came to him with a violent noise (painful for the Prophet); the angel was blowing into his heart; the angel came to him in the form of a man and spoke to him (easy for the Prophet); the angel came to him while he slept; or God spoke directly to him, either while he was awake or when he was sleeping.

The third and final question in this chapter on revelation deals with the interpretation of the famous hadith whose meaning remains disputed: "The Qur'an descended according to seven *harf.*" This hadith would mean that the Qur'an descended in seven variants. Suyûtî lists many interpretations but has some difficulty in positioning himself. These *harf* are not the "seven readings" (*qirâ'a*) recognized in the tenth century, he says. Rather, they would be "seven kinds of meanings, concordant with different words." For reasons of convenience, it was indeed possible at the beginning to replace a word of the Qur'an by another of the same meaning. But this permission would have been repealed eventually.

He concludes with a final remark, wondering whether the "'Uthmânic codices" included all seven *harf*. He leans rather toward the opinion that these codices contained only the *harf* whose consonantal *ductus* was admitted and which belonged to the final version that the Prophet would have submitted to Jibrîl. Against the first opinion, he reports the unanimity of "infallible" Companions around a single *harf* to unite the community. All the *harf* are therefore not present, but those that are are allowed because they appear in the final version that the Prophet submitted to Jibrîl. He claims that the Prophet had Jibrîl's reading of the Qur'an regularly checked, and that Zayd ibn Thâbit, the "redactor" of the Qur'an after Muhammad's death, had attended their last meeting. There has therefore been a limited plurality of "permitted" readings, but these no longer really make sense after the cultural development of Muslims. And in any case, the Companions "infallibly" agreed on one of them, which was corrected for the final edition.

PERSPECTIVE FROM CHRISTIANITY BY GERALD O'COLLINS

"Experience," "variety," "signs," "apologetics," and "new questions" could suggest some modalities of revelation in Islam that Jean-Marc Balhan's account brings up. Without developing a contemporary view of "experience," let alone attributing some philosophical/theological theory to any Islamic scholars, he could speak phenomenologically of their experiences and the "founding experiences of Judaism and Christianity." Among other things, he wanted to highlight the difference between the first historical experience of the Qur'an (as a recitation by particular people in a precise time and place) and the Qur'an as a written book bound between two covers.[64] Christian fundamental theologians may pick up these themes when they move through Balhan's rich account of the modalities of revelation in Islamic thought.

It is not that the *experiences* of Abraham, Jacob, Moses, and Jesus—to mention four of the Prophet's predecessors—feature as such in Islam's picture of revelation. At least in what Balhan reports, we do find Islamic theologians who have taken up and expounded the language of experience. When we speak of "the Qur'anic experience," we need not take sides in any controversy concerning such an all-pervasive reality. Yet "experience" could prove a fruitful theme for a comparative fundamental theology.

Many Christians, and specifically Catholic theologians and official teachers, however, avoided for years the noun or verb *experience* when expounding the divine communication to human beings. After eventually elaborating and publishing in November 1965 its Dogmatic Constitution on Divine Revelation (*Dei Verbum*), the Second Vatican Council (1962–65) used only cautiously such language of "experience" (8, 14). It was left to Pope John Paul II (pope 1978–2005) to talk without inhibition about the human experience of the divine self-revelation.[65] The official *Catechism of the Catholic Church*

DIVINE REVELATION according to CHRISTIANITY, JUDAISM, and ISLAM

(first published in 1992) implicitly endorsed this usage. It persistently cited the lived experience of saintly men and women whose faith embraced heroically the overtures of God's self-manifestation.

When preparing to publish in 1981 my first major work on divine revelation and its related themes, I took advantage of the elaboration of "experience" (as both *Erfahrung* and *Erleben*) in recent German philosophy. That philosophical presentation of "experience" has continued to throw light on aspects of divine revelation professed by Christian faith.[66]

Second, Balhan illustrates the *variety of mediators* and narratives of revelation accepted in Islamic theology—from Adam right through to Muhammad himself. Along with a variety of mediators, variety also characterizes the means and modalities of revelation that reach their highpoint with the Qur'an.

Revelation can come through dreams, miracles, and a range of signs in nature and history that Balhan goes out of his way to present in detail. Here Christian fundamental theologians could be reminded of the publications of the uncrowned dean of fundamental theology, René Latourelle (1918–2017). He explored extensively the saving and revealing function of such signs and attended, in particular, to miraculous signs. In Christianity as in Islam, miracles have attested and incorporated the divine self-disclosure.

Balhan shows how sinful human actions, even on the part of entire communities of people, may also be acknowledged in Islamic theology as occasions or even means of the divine revelation becoming known, albeit to be rejected by those whom God addresses. Not only individual sin (e.g., David's commission of adultery and the murder of Bathsheba's husband, Uriah) but also "social sin" may play a role in disclosing God's merciful designs for human beings.

From 1 Peter, the Acts of the Apostles and the second-century Justin Martyr, Christian thinkers have persistently set themselves to give an apologetic account of their hope (1 Pet 3:15). This brings us to a third aspect of Islamic theology that caught my attention in Balhan's chapter: *apologetics*. Merely human resources remain insuf-

THE MODALITIES OF REVELATION IN ISLAM

ficient to explain the origins of the Qur'an; Muhammad himself was illiterate.

A similar line of argument had been developed by Augustine of Hippo in his apologetic for accepting the crucified Christ's resurrection from the dead. Without invoking God's involvement and endorsement, Augustine claimed, we could not account for an "incredible" historical fact: "a few fishermen out on the sea of the world with the nets of faith, with no education in the liberal arts, completely untaught in the doctrines of pagan thought, not trained in *grammar*, not equipped with *dialectic*, not swollen with *rhetoric*," could manage to catch "all those fish of every kind."[67]

Balhan's chapter faced me with other questions about further areas of fundamental theology in which Christian (and Jewish) thinkers would want to enter into the positions and arguments of their Muslim counterparts. First, when cultural and social changes bring up new questions, what roles should the original written revelation and the successive religious traditions, respectively, play in handling and deciding on those issues? That issue emerges with a special force when one is faced with contemporary questions that seemingly cannot find any obvious place in the thinking of the Bible or the Qur'an.

Balhan cited the Islamic theme of God summoning everyone in "pre-eternity." Second, that summons reminded me of a key theme in the theology of Karl Rahner (1904–84), one of the most influential theological experts (*periti*) at Vatican II: the supernatural existential. By this Rahner intended a free (supernatural) divine call to share the eternal life of glory that is lodged in every human being even before they come into existence and begin a life also shaped by their free decisions. Does the summons in "pre-eternity" converge at all with the Rahnerian supernatural existence?

Third, Balhan dedicated space to "the *light* of Muhammad." Some Christian fundamental theologians have taken up the theme of "light" from the Gospel of John and other sources and shaped a fundamental theology around a Johannine scheme of the mutual inherence of revelatory light and salvific life. Is there any similar Islamic development to be invoked here?

All in all, Jean-Marc Balhan's chapter on the modalities of revelation in Islamic thought raised numerous questions for my own vision of fundamental theology. A common exploration of these questions promises to be seriously and mutually enlightening.

PERSPECTIVE FROM JUDAISM
BY MARC RASTOIN

Jean-Marc Balhan's presentation of revelation in Islam brings alive for readers, nourished by different traditions of the Abrahamic branch, an original experience of otherness. On the one hand, they hear terms that clearly recall what they know (or think they know!), such as *angel, scripture, prophet, judgment, traditions*, and even *signs* (as in the Gospel of John), and they perceive a thousand analogies. On the other hand, each time, differences in accent disorient them and force them to recognize that they are facing a new, although partly familiar, reality. A few theological motifs make it possible to touch this subtle mixture of known and original. The God who speaks is a God who calls for the receivers of revelation to become his "witnesses." Transcendent to the world he created, he necessarily passes through his creatures to be known. One can think of a famous midrash on the verse of Isaiah: "It is written, 'You are my witnesses,' said the Lord…'and I am God'" (Isa 43:10). That means: "If you testify to God's existence, he exists; if you do not, it is as if God does not exist" (*Sifré Devarim*, 346). In addition to the book of Scriptures, the perfect sign, there is also the book of Creation itself: "To those who are attentive and reflective, these signs reveal the goodness of creation and God's mercy," writes Balhan. This idea is found in both the Jewish and Christian traditions.

Another element is striking. Paradoxically, the affirmation of perfect revelation tends to give the prophet a decisive mediating role. Balhan refers to "the Prophet Muhammad and the first community of believers" and notes that believers "have access to it [the Scripture] only through the Prophet." It is impossible to separate faith in God *and* faith in his Messenger. Suffice it to quote the bold biblical verse, "the people feared the Lord, they put their faith in the Lord and in his servant Moses" (Exod 14:31), which concludes the crossing of

DIVINE REVELATION ACCORDING TO CHRISTIANITY, JUDAISM, AND ISLAM

the sea, the great sign performed by God for the people of Israel. How bold it is to insert this *and* which, at the same time, distinguishes faith in God and faith in his prophet but, at the same time, puts them, in a sense, on the same level. Theologically, monotheism necessarily introduces a complex system of mediations, angelic or prophetic, to try to reconcile inaccessibility and divine transcendence with its conversational proximity and insertion into history. It is a question of both expressing the inaccessible transcendence of God and the fact that he makes himself present, in a way that escapes representation, to his prophets and, through them, to humanity.

By the same logic, if it is common for the three traditions to insist on the perfect, absolute, and complete side of the moment of Revelation—whether to Moses at Mount Sinai, to Jesus as Son of God, or to the Prophet Muhammad in his time—there necessarily appears the need for a *tradition* that comes to explain and clarify the content of the luminous, too bright revelation. In the Jewish tradition, the notion of "Oral Law" (*Torah she-ba'al peh*) gradually imposed itself and crystallized in the Talmud while, in Christianity, the notion of Tradition also arose. Here, the collections of hadiths (the corpus of sayings and doings of the Prophet Muhammad) constituting the Sunna allow the subsequent tradition to radiate the unique and original moment of revelation. As with the Talmud, the sayings and doings were "first transmitted in oral form, and gradually written down and compiled into collections." Thus the text remains alive and the inspiration that animates it allows it to answer other questions (sometimes verbalizing what had remained implicit in the Revelation). We remember that "the Gospel" also does not designate first of all a *writing*, much less a set of writings, but a *message* proclaimed, as Paul often says. Here too, analogically, the Qur'an is a recitation marked by poetry and orality before being written down: "In the end," says Balhan, "the *qur'an* (recitation) thus also became a *kitâb*."

It is fascinating how each tradition contains texts about the celestial ascension of one or more personages. Balhan's reflections on the Qur'anic reserves about the notion of God's "descent" are thus evocative. In the New Testament we find Paul's account of how he was carried in ecstasy to the third heaven (2 Cor 12:1–6). But the New Testament goes very far in affirming that the "word of God" pitched his tent among human beings (John 1:14). We could mention so many similar themes such as the fact that "revelation begins in a certain sense, even before creation, in pre-eternity." Being able to speak of "the preexistence of this light of Muhammad" recalls "the light born of light" of the Council of Nicaea. For its part, a well-known midrash speaks of "things created before the foundation of the world," mentioning in the first place the Torah (*Beresheet Rabbah* 1,4; see also T.B. *Pesach'im* 54a and T.B. *Nedarim* 39b). This is to say that God's plan of salvation and communication comes from his very eternity.

A final point I note is the way in which tradition deals with the question of plurality. Despite colossal efforts to ensure a unique text and tightly controlled chains of transmission, diversity inevitably creeps in. Needless to say, there are four Gospels. Balhan evokes the question of the seven *harf* (letters) in the Muslim tradition. A *hadith* "tells us that 'Umar [one of the Prophet's Companions and future Caliph] heard someone recite a sura in a *harf* that he had never heard from the Messenger of God. 'Umar took him aside, and the Prophet asked them both to recite this sura. 'Although their recitations were different,' he said to each of them, 'it was sent down in this way.'"

How can we not think of the famous debate between the schools of Hillel and Shammai on a point of law? "Rabbi Aba said in the name of Samuel: for three years debate [*Machloket*] prevailed between the school of Hillel and the school of Shamai, each of them maintaining that *Halakha* should be fixed according to their opinion. A heavenly voice announced, 'These words and those words are the words of the living God, but it is *halacha* according to the school of Hillel that is the right one.'" And yet, if these like those are the words of the living God, why did Hillel's school have the merit of seeing the law fixed according to his opinion? Because they are "accommodating and humble, and they teach both their own opinions and those of the school of Shammai; and better still, they give precedence to the opinions of the school of Shammai over their own" (Talmud *Bavli*, *Eruvin* 13b). May this spirit of discussion and respect develop *between* religions as well as *within* the religions themselves!

EPILOGUE

Gerald O'Collins

Three chapters (written by O'Collins, Rastoin, and Balhan, respectively) provide the heart of this book—the accounts that Christianity, Judaism, and Islam offer to issues treated by fundamental theology (revelation, tradition, and the inspired Scriptures). The conversation among these three monotheistic faiths that each claim a heritage from Abraham features significant similarities: for instance, a conviction that faith in God is inseparable from faith in the envoys (who play a major, even unique, role of envoys) or at least in the Envoy (in upper case); and the need to discern traditions that interpret and apply the original revelation.

Each of the three chapters enjoys a pair of responses that embody various suggestions and reminders. The responses can enrich or at least clarify any teaching on revelation according to Christianity, Judaism, and Islam. Let me take up three examples, all from Rastoin, and close with a story about the "rosary" of ninety-nine beads that Muslim believers use when meditating on the Most Excellent Names of God.

First, in commenting on my chapter, Rastoin rightly notes how the narrative theology of faith that I develop privileges a Johannine, "individualistic" approach. Judaism suggests a qualification. Its account of divine revelation highlights how God, albeit regularly through individual "envoys," addressed primarily the people and the community.

DIVINE REVELATION according to CHRISTIANITY, JUDAISM, and ISLAM

That reminder suggests to me a call for Christian theology to explore the Book of Acts and, specifically, Luke's account of groups accepting in faith and through the power of the Holy Spirit the self-disclosure of God in the crucified and resurrected Jesus. Such Christian theology of the faith that responds to divine revelation might also incorporate what can be gleaned from the letters of Paul about communities opening themselves to God's word. Here a comparative theology could provide a narrative of faith that matches more successfully the place of the people and the community in Judaism.

Second, when reading Rastoin's response to Balhan's chapter, I found another personal corrective in the former's words about "the incessant rabbinical ability to privilege the question over the answer." It is not that I neglected the questions; they turn up in a section of my chapter above when I present the human condition. But my questions emerge from the book of creation, especially those that come from children, works of art, and some forms of psychotherapy. Such questions should be heard, but we should also give proper weight to the questions raised by the book of the Bible.

One must dive deeply when reflecting on God's words to Adam, "where are you?" (Gen 3:9). Where, indeed, have Adam and his partner been taken through disobeying the divine command? Where does such sinful disobedience place human beings in their relationship with God who is set on showering them with blessing upon blessing?

We may call the Scriptures "the word of God," even while we remember that the divine word often takes the form of questions. When speaking to Job out of the whirlwind, God declares: "I will question you and you will answer me" (Job 38:3). This extraordinary drama, concerned with the testing of a man of faith, ends with four chapters that evoke the limitations in the knowledge and power of human beings (Job 38—42). The interaction between God and Job could be expressed by adapting Gerard Manley Hopkins's opening lines for "The Wreck of the Deutschland": "Thou questioning me / God!"

EPILOGUE

The Fourth Gospel is punctuated by questions put by Jesus from start to finish: "What are you looking for?" (John 1:38) to the only question he repeats three times—"Do you love me?" (John 21:15–17). More than any other book of the New Testament, the Gospel according to John endorses the title "Jesus the Questioner."

Third and finally, Rastoin opens his response to Balhan with a "warning" about such familiar terms as *scripture*, *prophet*, and *signs*. Reflecting on Abrahamic traditions other their own, Christian, Jewish, and Muslim scholars forget at their peril that they face "a new, although partly familiar, reality."

But rather than end by underscoring difficulties, Rastoin recalls a famous three-year debate between the schools of Hillel and Shammai. God intervened to ensure that a spirit of discussion marked by respect developed. Rastoin prays that "this spirit of discussion and respect develop *between religions* as well as *within* the religions themselves!"

This hope echoes some words of Pope John XXIII, a great friend of Jews and Muslims alike: "Those things which unite the faithful are stronger than those which divide them. Let there be unity in what is necessary, freedom in what is doubtful, and charity in everything."[1]

When Balhan (in his response to my chapter above) described the function in Islamic prayer of the ninety-nine Names of God, I found myself recalling a painful incident in Catholic-Muslim relations from many years ago. It concerned Muslim asylum seekers detained by Australian authorities on Christmas Island in the Indian Ocean. I lent my support to a kindly woman who supplied the Muslims with rosaries of ninety-nine beads that enabled them to invoke God as encouraged by the Qur'an. The member of a local archdiocese reported me to the Catholic archbishop who seemed to find something objectionable in my encouraging Muslims to pray. The dictum quoted from St. Augustine by Pope John XXIII ("unity in what is necessary, freedom in what is doubtful, and charity in everything") lent its support then to my decision and continues to do so.

NOTES

CHAPTER 1

1. Wolfson had published *Philo: Foundations of Religious Philosophy in Judaism, Christianity, Islam* (Cambridge, MA: Harvard University Press, 1962). Wolfson argued that Philo developed philosophical principles that became the common foundations of Judaism, Christianity, and Islam. As a background to the three Abrahamic religions, see Michael Barnes, *Interreligious Learning: Dialogue, Spirituality and the Christian Imagination* (Cambridge: Cambridge University Press, 2012).

2. See D. Burrell, *Towards a Jewish-Christian-Muslim Theology* (Oxford: Wiley-Blackwell, 2011).

3. *Tesi gregoriana: serie teologica* 103 (Rome: Editrice Pontificia Università, 2004).

4. *Tesi gregoriana: serie teologica* 297–322.

5. G. O'Collins, D. Kendall, and G. LaBelle, eds., *Pope John Paul II: A Reader* (Mahwah, NJ: Paulist Press, 2007).

6. G. O'Collins and Michael A. Hayes, eds., *The Legacy of John Paul II* (London: Burns & Oates, 2008).

7. G. O'Collins, *The Second Vatican Council on Other Religions* (Oxford: Oxford University Press, 2012); see G. O'Collins, "The Second Vatican Council on Other Religions Revisited," *New Blackfriars* 103 (2022): 597–606.

8. G. O'Collins, *Salvation for All: God's Other Peoples* (Oxford: Oxford University Press, 2008).

9. G. O'Collins, *Rethinking Fundamental Theology* (Oxford: Oxford University Press, 2011), 334–36. Gilbert Narcisse insists that all theologians who "deal with revelation must clarify" their "philosophical position" (OHDivRev, 165).

10. L. Wittgenstein, *Culture and Value*, trans. Peter Winch (Oxford: Basil Blackwell, 1980), 32c, 33c; both passages are quoted by O'Collins, *Easter Faith* (London: Darton, Longman & Todd, 2003), 66, 107.

11. *Atheism and Christianity: The Religion of the Exodus and Christianity*, trans. J. T. Swann (London: Verso Books, 2009; German orig., 1968).

12. *Scottish Journal of Theology* 21 (1968): 129–44.

13. G. O'Collins, *Man and His New Hopes* (New York: Herder and Herder, 1969).

14. Gerhard von Rad (1901–71) reacted to Nazi anti-Semitism by proposing the message of the Old Testament and so preparing the post–World War II blossoming of Old Testament studies in Germany and beyond.

15. B. Mezei et al., eds., *Oxford Handbook of Divine Revelation* (Oxford: Oxford University Press, 2021), xxiii; emphasis added.

16. For difficulties against faith in God, see Tina Beattie, *The New Atheists: The Twilight of Reason and the War on Religion* (London: Darton, Longman & Todd, 2007); Michael J. Buckley, *At the Origins of Modern Atheism* (New Haven, CT: Yale University Press, 1990); Sarah Coakley, *Sacrifice Regained: Reconsidering the Rationality of Religious Belief* (Cambridge: Cambridge University Press, 2011); John Cottingham, *Why Believe?* (London: Continuum, 2009); David Ferguson, *Faith and Its Critics: A Conversation* (Oxford: Oxford University Press, 2009); George Karuvelil, *Faith, Reason and Culture: An Essay in Fundamental Theology* (Cham, Switzerland: Palgrave Macmillan, 2020); John Lennox, *God's Undertaker: Has Science Buried God?* (Oxford: Liam Hudson, 2007); Eric Reitan, *Is God a Delusion? A Reply to Religion's Cultured Despisers* (Oxford: Wiley-Blackwell, 2009); Rupert Shortt, *Outgrowing Dawkins* (London: SPCK, 2019);

Charles Taylor, *A Secular Age* (Cambridge, MA: Harvard University Press, 2007); James E. Taylor, "Revelation and the New Atheism," OHDivRev, 322–37.

17. C. Hitchens, *God Is Not Great: How Religion Poisons Everything* (London: Atlantic Books, 2008); R. Dawkins, *The God Delusion* (London: Transworld Publishers, 2006).

18. S. Freud, *The Future of an Illusion*, trans. James Strachey (New York: Norton, 1961; orig. German, 1927), 54. I confronted this statement in *Fundamental Theology* (New York: Paulist Press, 1981), 32.

19. G. O'Collins, *Moments of Grace: Daily Inspiration from Isaiah to Revelation* (Buxhall, Sussex: Kevin Mayhew, 2018), 74–75; O'Collins, *Pause for Thought: Making Time for Prayer, Jesus, and God* (Mahwah, NJ: Paulist Press, 2011), 51–52.

20. S. Freud, *Civilization and Its Discontents*, trans. James Strachey (New York: Norton, 1961; orig. German, 1930), 57.

21. 5th ed., Michael Coogan, ed. (New York: Oxford University Press, 2018).

22. See John Butt, "George Friedric Handel and *The Messiah*," in *Oxford Handbook of the Reception History of the Bible*, ed. Michael Lieb et al. (Oxford: Oxford University Press, 2011), 294–306.

23. R. Otto, *The Idea of the Holy*, trans. John W. Harvey (Oxford: Oxford University Press, 1973; German orig., 1917).

24. See G. O'Collins, *Inspiration: Towards a Christian Interpretation of Biblical Inspiration* (Oxford: Oxford University Press, 2018), 27–32.

25. D. Gascoyne, *Collected Poems* (Oxford: Oxford University Press, 1965), 44–46. He quotes here from Blaise Pascal, *Pensées*, trans. W. F. Trotter (Mineola, NY: Dover Publications, 2003), 148.

26. Trans. Stella Rodway (New York: Hill and Wang, 1960; orig. Yiddish, 1956).

27. Robert Coles, in *The Spiritual Life of Children* (Oxford: Blackwell, 1990), shows how children ponder the great questions about our origin, our nature, and our final destiny.

28. Mezei et al., *Oxford Handbook of Divine Revelation*.

29. Norman Solomon, "Revelation in the Jewish Tradition," in Mezei et al., *Oxford Handbook of Divine Revelation*, 371–90; Nader El-Bizri. "Divine Revelation in Islam," in Mezei et al., *Oxford Handbook of Divine Revelation*, 391–403.

30. Wolfhart Pannenberg names Friedrich Schelling (1775–1854) as having introduced the expression *self-revelation* (*Selbstoffenbarung*), traces the notion back to Philo and Plotinus, and cites Aquinas, Bonaventure, Cajetan, and Hegel as proposing a divine self-revelation without using the precise term; see Pannenberg, "Offenbarung und Offenbarungen im Zeugnis der Geschichte," in *Handbuch der Fundamentaltheologie*, vol. 2, ed. Walter Kern et al. (Tübingen: Francke, 2000), 63–82, at 78–81.

31. Karl Rahner, *Foundations of Christian Faith: An Introduction to the Idea of Christianity*, trans. William V. Dych (New York: Seabury Press, 1978), 44–89.

32. Gregory of Nyssa, *Life of Moses*, 11.163, trans. Abraham J. Malherbe, Classics of Western Spirituality (New York: Paulist Press, 1978), 95; see Daniel Howard-Snyder and Paul K. Moser, eds., *Divine Hiddenness* (Cambridge: Cambridge University Press, 2002).

33. K. Bailey, *The Middle-Eastern Jesus* (London: SPCK, 2008); R. Bauckham, *Jesus and the Eyewitnesses: The Gospels as Eyewitness Testimony*, 2nd ed. (Grand Rapids, MI: Eerdmans, 2017); J. D. G. Dunn, *Christianity in the Making*, vol. 1, *Jesus Remembered* (Grand Rapids, MI: Eerdmans, 2003); P. R. Eddy and G. Boyd, *The Jesus Legend: A Case for the Historical Reliability of the Synoptic Jesus Tradition* (Grand Rapids, MI: Baker Academic, 2007); M. Hengel and A. M. Schwemer, *Jesus and Judaism*, trans. Wayne Coppins (Waco, TX: Baylor University Press, 2019); C. S. Keener, *The Historical Jesus of the Gospels* (Grand Rapids, MI: Eerdmans, 2009); G. Lohfink, *Jesus of Nazareth: What He Wanted, Who He Was*, trans. Linda M. Maloney (Collegeville, MN: Liturgical Press, 2015); J. P. Meier, *A Marginal Jew: Rethinking the Historical Jesus*, vols. 1–3 (New York: Doubleday, 1991–2001), vols. 4–5 (New Haven, CT: Yale University Press,

2009–19); G. O'Collins, *Jesus: A Portrait* (London: Darton, Longman & Todd, 2008); D. Wenham, *Jesus in Context: Making Sense of the Historical Figure* (Oxford: Oxford University Press, 2022).

34. J. Marcus, *Mark 1—8* (New York: Doubleday, 2000) and *Mark 8—16* (New Haven, CT: Yale University Press, 2009); U. Luz, *Matthew*, 3 vols. (Minneapolis: Fortress Press, 2001); F. Bovon, *Luke: A Commentary*, 3 vols. (Minneapolis: Fortress Press, 2002–12).

35. See G. O'Collins, *Revelation: Towards a Christian Interpretation of God's Self-Revelation in Jesus Christ* (Oxford: Oxford University Press, 2016), 108–10.

36. See G. O'Collins, *Jesus Risen: An Historical, Fundamental and Systematic Examination of Christ's Resurrection* (Mahwah, NJ: Paulist Press, 1987); O'Collins, *Easter Faith: Believing in the Risen Jesus* (London: Darton, Longman & Todd, 2003); O'Collins, *Believing in the Resurrection: The Meaning and Promise of the Risen Jesus* (Mahwah, NJ: Paulist Press, 2012).

37. P. Winter, *On the Trial of Jesus* (Berlin: Walter de Gruyter, 1961).

38. Winter, *On the Trial of Jesus*, 149; see O'Collins, *Jesus Risen*, 103–7; O'Collins, *Believing in the Resurrection*, 47–60.

39. G. Vermès, *Jesus a Jew: A Historian's Reading* (London: Collins, 1973); see O'Collins, *Believing in the Resurrection*, 20–22.

40. *The Resurrection of Jesus: A Jewish Perspective*, trans. Wilhelm C. Linss (Eugene, OR: Wipf & Stock, 2002; German orig. 1977).

41. D. Cohn-Sherbok, "The Resurrection of Jesus: A Jewish View," in *Resurrection Reconsidered*, ed. Gavin D'Costa (Oxford: Oneworld, 1996), 184–200, at 198.

42. Most scholars agree that the episode of the woman taken in adultery was inserted later in the Fourth Gospel. Yet it witnesses, in its own and vivid fashion, to the historical Jesus's way of acting; see A. T. Lincoln, *The Gospel According to John* (London: Continuum, 2005), 524–36.

43. Some commentators interpret the Samaritan woman merely symbolically: her "marital" relationships refer simply to

gods worshipped by the Samaritans. Lincoln argues that "there is no need to choose between a more literal or a more symbolic interpretation." The symbolic interpretation, if it is "to work effectively," needs the literal interpretation "in which the woman is viewed as morally suspect." The symbolic meaning for Lincoln concerns above all a betrothal scene, in which Christ as bridegroom seeks his bride, the new people of God (*The Gospel According to John*, 170, 172–74, 176).

44. On faith in Hebrews, see C. R. Koester, *Hebrews* (New York: Doubleday, 2003), 468–553; on applying to "other" believers what Hebrews say about faith, see O'Collins, *Revelation*, 200–201.

45. O'Collins, *Revelation*, 1–18.

46. O'Collins, *Revelation*, 183–204.

47. O'Collins, *Revelation*, 101–20.

48. O'Collins, *Revelation*, 121–45; see O'Collins, *Tradition: Understanding Christian Tradition* (Oxford: Oxford University Press, 2018).

49. See the judicious concluding remarks of Arie W. Zwiep, *The Ascension of the Messiah in Lukan Christology* (Leiden: Brill, 1997).

50. See the suggestive articles by Jean-Pierre Sonnet on this subject: "Between Poetic Justice and Poetic Mercy: God in the Flood Narrative (Gen 6—7)," *Nova et Vetera* 18 (2020): 1247–65 ; Sonnet, "God's Repentance and 'False Starts' in Biblical History (Genesis 6—9; Exodus 32—34; 1 Samuel 15; and 2 Samuel 7)," in *Congress Volume: Ljubljana 2007*, ed. André Lemaire (Boston: Brill, 2010), 469–94; Sonnet, "The Divine Monologues in the Pentateuch: A Shakespearean God?," in *The Vita Benedetta*, ed. Fabrizio Ficco (Rome: Gregorian Biblical Press, 2018).

51. Benjamin D. Sommer, *The Bodies of God and the World of Ancient Israel* (New York: Cambridge University Press, 2009). See also his *Revelation and Authority: Sinai in Jewish Scripture and Tradi-*

tion (New Haven, CT: Yale University Press, 2015). The fruitfulness of these readings for a Christian theology appears, for example, in Nathan Chambers, "Reading Joshua with Augustine and Sommer: Two Frameworks for Interpreting Theophany Narrative," *JSOT* 43 (2019): 273–83.

52. Steven Harvey, "The Changing Image of al-Ghazâlî in Medieval Jewish Thought," in *Islam and Rationality: The Impact of al-Ghazālī. Papers Collected on His 900th Anniversary*, vol. 1, ed. Georges Tanner (Leiden: Brill, 2015), 288–302.

53. See, e.g., the publications of Angelika Neuwirth, in particular, *The Qur'an and Late Antiquity: A Shared Heritage* (Oxford: Oxford University Press, 2019).

54. See Michel Younès, *Les approches chrétiennes de l'islam. Tensions, déplacements, enjeux* (Paris: Cerf, 2020).

55. For a good summary of Muslim theology, in particular as found in the last decades, see Rotraud Wielandt, "Main Trends of Islamic, Theological Thought from the Late Nineteenth Century to Present Times," in *The Oxford Handbook of Islamic Theology*, ed. Sabine Schmidtke (Oxford: Oxford University Press, 2016), 707–64.

56. For more on this, see Angelika Neuwirth, "From Tribal Genealogy to Divine Covenant: Qur'anic Reconfigurations of Pagan Arab Ideals Based on Biblical Models," in A. Neuwirth, *Scripture, Poetry and the Making of a Community: Reading the Qur'an as a Literary Text* (Oxford: Oxford University Press, 2014), 53–75.

57. See Thomas Sizgorich, *Violence and Belief in Late Antiquity: Militant Devotion in Christianity and Islam* (Philadelphia: University of Pennsylvania Press, 2009); and Michael Gaddis, *There Is No Crime for Those Who Have Christ: Religious Violence in the Christian Roman Empire* (Berkeley: University of California Press, 2005).

58. Shahab Ahmad, *What Is Islam: The Importance of Being Islamic* (Princeton, NJ: Princeton University Press, 2015).

59. See n55 above.

DIVINE REVELATION according to
CHRISTIANITY, JUDAISM, and ISLAM

CHAPTER 2

1. See Daniel Boyarin, *Judaism: The Genealogy of a Modern Notion* (New Brunswick, NJ: Rutgers University Press, 2019), who notes: "For both Zionists and many non-Zionist Jews (including me), versions of description or practice with respect to Judaism that treat it as a faith that can be separated from ethnicity, nationality, language and shared history have felt false" (153). See also, in more polemical manner, Daniel Dubuisson, *The Invention of Religions*, trans. Martha Cunningham (Sheffield: Equinox Publishing, 2019).

2. Adin Steinsaltz, *We Jews: Who Are We and What Should We Do?*, trans. Yehuda Hanegbi and Rebecca Toueg (San Francisco: Jossey-Bass, 2005).

3. See Alan F. Segal, *Rebecca's Children: Judaism and Christianity in the Roman World* (Cambridge, MA: Harvard University Press, 1986).

4. See Daniel Boyarin, *Border Lines: The Partition of Judaeo-Christianity* (Philadelphia: University of Pennsylvania Press, 2004).

5. This point of view is notably defended by the French specialist on the second temple, André Paul, *Leçons paradoxales sur les juifs et les chrétiens* (Paris: Desclée de Brouwer, 1992).

6. Without neglecting the supreme divine freedom, the Jewish tradition, like the Catholic tradition, emphasizes the freedom of the act of faith and the free will; this is seen in such maxims as "Everything is in the hands of God except the fear of God" (*Bavli, Berakhot* 33b); "everything is foreseen yet freedom of choice is granted; the world is judged with goodness; and everything is in accordance with the preponderance of works" (*Pirkei Avot* 3.15).

7. The Old Testament of the Christian Bible is larger than the Hebrew Bible because it includes several books written in Greek according to the canon of the Jews of Alexandria.

8. See Daniel Boyarin, *A Traveling Homeland: The Babylonian Talmud as Diaspora* (Philadelphia: University of Pennsylvania Press, 2015).

9. See Hannah Hashkes, *Rabbinic Discourse as a System of Knowledge* (Leiden: Brill, 2015).

10. On this point see the very enlightening works of the historian Erich Gruen, *Heritage and Hellenism: The Rejuvenation of Jewish Tradition* (Berkeley: University of California Press, 1998); and Gruen, *Diaspora: Jews amidst Greeks and Romans* (Cambridge, MA: Harvard University Press, 2002).

11. See the interesting collective work, *Judaisms and Their Messiahs at the Turn of the Christian Era*, ed. Jacob Neusner, William Scott Green, and Ernest S. Frerichs (Cambridge: Cambridge University Press, 1988).

12. If modern Zionism, born at the end of the nineteenth century, is a modern phenomenon comparable to the "lay" European nationalisms of the period, one must not forget that there have always been Jewish communities living in the land of Israel, other Jews who wanted to live in that land, and Jews who succeeded in returning to that land. The creation of the state of Israel in 1948 has divided the Jewish religious world between Zionists and anti-Zionists (a very small minority today), adding a further criterion of distinction at its heart. On this point see a very complete work by Yakov Rabkin, *Au nom de la Torah: une histoire de l'opposition juive au sionisme* (Quebec: Presses de l'université de Laval, 2004); and Aviezer Revitzky, *Messianism, Zionism, and Jewish Religious Radicalism*, trans. Michael Swirsky and Jonathan Chipman (Chicago: University of Chicago Press, 1996).

13. The notion of "Christian atheist" is a contradiction in terms in a way, then, astonishing as it can be for Christians, that "Jewish atheist" is not. Certainly, it is legitimate to ask whether that situation can endure over time, but it is not an aberration.

14. Rabbi David Berger, in his important work *The Rebbe, the Messiah and the Scandal of Orthodox Indifference* (Oxford: Littman

Library of Jewish Civilization, 2001), has criticized the position of certain Lubavitcher Jews who consider the leader, Rabbi Menahem Schneerson (1902–94), to be the Messiah. Following the line that "some among them have very bizarre, even totally, heterodox ideas on God, while their practice is correct," Berger has seen that the axiom was sufficiently powerful to back the demand for the condemnation of that current of Hassidic Judaism which orthodox American rabbis view as having run aground. In the year 2000, he also published an important declaration on the document *Dabru Emet*: "Statement by Dr. David Berger Regarding the *New York Times* advertisement by *Dabru Emet*."

15. The very fact of distinguishing between ritual commandments and ethical commandments is itself a typically Christian manner of seeing things. In Romans and Galatians, Paul engages in abundant polemic against the "works of the law," aiming essentially at the ritual commandments, as the New Perspective on Paul shows.

16. A second Talmud exists—the Jerusalem Talmud or of the land of Israel—which is a little shorter and earlier. But it does not have the same legal authority as the Babylonian Talmud.

17. Theoretically the written Torah has greater authority. But the oral Torah is equally authoritative and is inseparable from the written text as its legitimate interpretation. Within the oral tradition there exists, besides, a hierarchy in what is considered fundamental and consensual.

18. To be sure, both the Sadducees and the Karaites had oral interpretations of the written Law. It is impossible to apply the biblical law without that type of complements, precisions, and so forth. But debate centered more on what determines the interpretation of the Scriptures. In this case, both challenged the rabbis' authority or their exclusive role.

19. This is rather similar to the way in which tradition functions in the Catholic Church: the Church is founded on Scripture, but the Church has determined the *content* of the canon and said

how to read it. Thus some passages are not quite simply read (or disactivated to be read in that way) like 1 Tim 2:15, for example.

20. This is the theme that provided the heart of the film *Kadosh* (1999) by the Israeli director Amos Gitai.

21. In a certain way, it is a little like canon *law* being at least as important as the *catechism*—to speak in Catholic categories.

22. See Avraham Yaakov Finkel, *Ein Yaakov: The Ethical and Inspirational Teachings of the Talmud* (Lanham, MD: Jason Aronson, 1999).

23. See Menachem Kellner, *Must a Jew Believe Anything?* (Liverpool: Littman Library of Jewish Civilisation, 1999).

24. See Moses Maimonides, *The Guide of the Perplexed*, ed. and trans. Shlomo Pinès (Chicago: University of Chicago Press, 1963).

25. This may seem very obvious, but the biblical text is far from clear on this point and can open the way to the notion of the "glorious body" of God; see the major work by Benjamin Sommer, *The Bodies of God and the World of Ancient Israel* (Cambridge: Cambridge University Press, 2009). Here Maimonides replies to contemporary Christian theologians.

26. The Talmudic discussion of Messianism (*Sanhedrin* 97a–99b) is notoriously complex and has been subject to different interpretations about the identity of the Messiah, the messianic times, and the nature of the end of the world. This diversity has rightly caused the position of Maimonides, which was probably only of a tactical order, to be controversial. His formulation leaves open the role of angels or intercessors, while making it clear that prayer can be addressed only to God. In Christian terms, this is comparable to the distinction between *latria* and *dulia*.

27. Maimonides was strongly criticized by several major rabbis between the twelfth and sixteenth centuries, including Abraham ben David of Posquières, Hasdai Crescas (whose work *Or Adonai—the Light of the Lord* provides six fundamental principles of Jewish faith), Joseph Albo, and Isaac Abarbanel—whatever one makes of his definition of the nature and number of dogmas. But the author of the

famous code *Choulhan âroukh*, Joseph Caro (1488–1575), declined to retain Maimonides's profession of dogmatic faith.

28. Robert Jenson, *Systematic Theology*, 2 vols. (Oxford: Oxford University Press, 1997–99), I: 63.

29. The account in Baba Metsia 59b of the excommunication of Rabbi Eliezer ben Hyrcanus demonstrates that a mystical experience—or a "voice from heaven"—could not supplant the rabbis' shared legal and rational discernment: see https://torahinmotion.org/discussions-and-blogs/bava-metzia-59-torah-is-not-in-heaven. A rabbi Eliezer invoked a heavenly voice to support his legal position, which all the other rabbis rejected. He worked miracles but the rabbis retorted: "the Torah is not in heaven." That is to say, henceforth it belongs to the rabbis on earth to fix the contours for the discussion and vote.

30. See Gershom Scholem, *Major Trends in Jewish Mysticism* (New York: Schocken Books, 1941).

31. Forced converts were known as *anusim*, in contradistinction to *meshumadim*, who had voluntarily left Judaism. For *anusim* alone a return to the community was possible, in line with the teaching: "All Israel have a share in the world to come" (*Pirkei Avot* 1.1).

32. See Y. Leibowitz, *Israel et judaisme: ma part de vérité*, ed. and trans. Gérard Haddad (Paris: Desclée de Brouwer, 1993), 103.

33. See Moshe Pelli, *The Age of Haskalah: Studies in Hebrew Literature of the Enlightenment in Germany* (Leiden: Brill, 1979).

34. See Franz Rosenzweig, *The Star of Redemption*, ed. and trans. Barbara Galli (Madison: University of Wisconsin Press, 2005).

35. Buber's book, ed. and trans. Ronald Gregor Smith (New York: Simon & Schuster, 1996; orig. 1923) had a big influence on Christian philosophy and theology in the twentieth century.

36. See the remarkable presentation of his life's journey in Ami Bouganim, *Joseph B. Soloveitchik: le maître de la Loi* (Nadir, 2000); his major work is *The Halakhic Mind* (Jewish Publication Society, 1984). See also Heshey Zelcer and Mark Zelcer, *The Philosophy of Joseph B. Soloveitchik* (London: Routledge, 2021).

37. Abraham Joshua Heschel, *The Sabbath* (New York: Farrar, Straus and Giroux, 1951). One should also mention his twin works: *Man Is Not Alone: A Philosophy of Religion* (Melrose Park, PA: Jewish Publication Society of America, 1951), and *God in Search of Man: A Philosophy of Judaism* (New York: Farrar, Straus and Giroux, 1955).

38. *Heavenly Torah: As Refracted through the Generations*, ed. and trans. Gordon Tucker (London: Continuum, 2006); for my part, I have read only this synthesis which has been made in English, an extraordinary work of introduction and translation. The first two volumes of *Torah min Hashamaim* were published in 1962; the third volume was published posthumously in 1995.

39. The masterpiece by E. Przywara is his 1932 work Analogia Entis*: Metaphysics, Original Structure and Universal Rhythm*, trans. John R. Betz and David Bentley Hart (Grand Rapids, MI: Eerdmans, 2014), along with *An Augustine Synthesis* (Eugene, OR: Wipf and Stock, 2014; orig., 1934).

40. *Heavenly Torah*, 33–34.

41. G. O'Collins, *Tradition: Understanding Christian Tradition* (Oxford: Oxford University Press, 2018).

42. Martin Davie et al., eds., *New Dictionary of Theology*, 2nd ed. (Downers Grove, IL: InterVarsity Press, 2016).

43. E. Shils, *Tradition* (London: Faber & Faber, 1980).

44. O'Collins, *Tradition*, 125–38.

45. B. Schwarz, *Abraham Lincoln and the Forge of National Memory* (Chicago: University of Chicago Press, 2000), x, xi.

46. See O'Collins, *Tradition*, 128–38.

47. On this subject see Claude Gilliot, "La vision de Dieu dans l'au-delà. Exégèse, tradition et théologie en islam," in *Pensée grecque et sagesse d'Orient. Hommage à Michel Tardieu*, ed. M. A. Amir-Moezzi et al. (Turnhout: Brepols, 2009), 239–60.

48. Quoted by Serge de Beaurecueil, "La mystique musulmane," in *Aspects de la foi de l'islam*, ed. Jacques Berque et al. (Brussels: Presses universitaires Saint-Louis, 1985), 121–48.

49. See Daniel Gimaret, *Les noms divins en Islam* (Paris: Cerf, 1988).

50. To enrich this reflection, see Souâd Ayada, *L'islam des théophanies. Une religion à l'epreuve de l'art* (Paris: CNRS Editions, 2010).

CHAPTER 3

1. In order not to make the text too heavy, and to make this chapter accessible to non-specialists, we have chosen to omit Hegirian dates and mention only the dating of the Christian era.

2. To make this chapter accessible to the non-specialist, we have chosen to adopt a simplified transliteration of Arabic, without diacritical points, but featuring the *'ayn* and also sometimes the *hamza* (not at the beginning of a word), as well as long vowels (*â, î, û*). For words that have passed into everyday language, we will use the usual English spelling, e.g., Qur'an, hadith, Sufi.

3. All the references to the Qur'an that feature in this chapter will be drawn from the English translation by M. A. S. Abdel Haleem, *The Qur'an* (Oxford: Oxford University Press, 2005; hereafter Q), which we have, nevertheless, reworked fairly often to make it more literal.

4. We do not add notes for all the technical terms. In general, we direct readers to two reference encyclopedias: P. Bearman et al., eds., *Encyclopedia of Islam*, 12 vols. (2nd ed. Leiden: Brill, 1960–2009; hereafter EI); and J. D. McAuliffe, ed., *Encyclopedia of the Qur'ān*, 5 vols. (Leiden: Brill, 2001–6; hereafter EQ).

5. On the evolution of the Muslim interpretation of the Qur'anic notion of the "falsification" of previous scriptures over the course of time—an alteration of the meaning or of the text itself, see Hava Lazarus-Yafeh, "Tahrîf," EI, vol. 10, 112–13.

6. In this chapter we present principally the traditional Muslim vision and its sources. For a historical and literary approach of the Qur'anic experience situated in its context by a scholar of Islamic studies, see the work of Angelica Neuwirth—in particular, *The Qur'an and Late Antiquity. A Shared Heritage* (Oxford: Oxford University Press, 2019). For a preliminary introduction, see Nicolai Sinai, *The Qur'an: A Historical-Critical Introduction* (Edinburgh: Edinburgh University Press, 2017).

7. The origin of this word is disputed; it probably comes from a word of Syrian origin, *surtâ*, meaning "writing." See Arthur Jeffery, *The Foreign Vocabulary of the Qur'an* (Baroda: Oriental Institute, 1938), 181–82.

8. This will be the point of departure for the doctrine of the Qur'an being inimitable, which begins to be elaborated two centuries later; see "The Miracle of the Inimitability of the Qur'an" later in this chapter.

9. The self-referential nature of the Qur'an and, in this setting, the manner in which it explains "revelation" have been studied in recent years by several scholars of Islamic studies. I mention here Daniel A. Madigan, *The Qur'an's Self-Image: Writing and Authority in Islam's Scripture* (Princeton, NJ: Princeton University Press, 2002), and especially Simon P. Loynes, *Revelation in the Qur'an. A Semantic Study of the Roots n-z-l and w-h-y* (Leiden: Brill, 2021), from which I draw in this section, taking up his thesis of a sharp division in meaning between the two roots *n-z-l* and *w-h-y*.

10. See, e.g., the section on "The Revelation of the Qur'an according to Suyûtî" in the end of this chapter.

11. Loynes, *Revelation in the Qur'an*, 63–70.

12. See the section on "The Sîra of the Prophet" in this chapter.

13. Loynes, *Revelation in the Qur'an*, 81.

14. Loynes, *Revelation in the Qur'an*, 87.

15. See the explanatory scheme of Loynes, *Revelation in the Qur'an*, 140.

16. Loynes, *Revelation in the Qur'an*, 143.

17. See, e.g., the section on "The Revelation of the Qur'an according to Suyûtî" in the end of this chapter.
18. Loynes, *Revelation in the Qur'an*, 146.
19. For example, the English translation that we use by Abdel Haleem mentions this in a note; see *The Qur'an*, 237, 429.
20. See Eric Geoffroy, "Ummî," EI, vol. 10, 863–64.
21. See the section on "Revelation in the Sunna" in this chapter.
22. Historically speaking, the process was not that simple; for a long time, variants were in circulation. That said, the text of the most ancient manuscripts, whose writing is still deficient, dates from the end of the seventh century and is compatible with the canonical version that we read today. See the works of François Déroche bearing on the first manuscripts of the Qur'an.
23. This was done at the initiative of Ibn Mujâhid (d. 936). In our time the most widespread version is that of Hafs according to 'Âsim, which one finds in the Cairo edition (1924), available now in the whole world and thus realizing the ambition of Caliph 'Uthmân.
24. For a general introduction to the Hadith, see Jonathan A. C. Brown, *Hadith: Muhammad's Legacy in the Medieval and Modern World* (London: Oneworld, 2009).
25. See Jonathan A. C. Brown, *The Canonization of al-Bukhârî and Muslim: The Formation and Function of the Sunnî Hadîth Canon* (Leiden: Brill, 2007).
26. *Sahîh al-Bukhârî*, Arabic-English, trans. Muhammad Muhsin Khan, 9 vols. (Riyadh: Darussalam Publishers, 1997), 1: 46–47; we alter the translation of this and following passages.
27. *Sahîh al-Bukhârî*, 6: 431.
28. See, e.g., the section on "The Revelation of the Qur'an according to Suyûtî" in the end of this chapter.
29. *Sahîh al-Bukhârî*, 6: 427–29.
30. It is based on the dialect of Quraysh, for according to this hadith and others, the Qur'an came down in this dialect.

NOTES

31. Shâfi'î, *La Risâla, les fondements du droit musulman*, trans. from Arabic, presented and annotated by Lakhdar Souami (Paris: Sindbad, Actes Sud, 1997), # 244, 252, 257, pp. 92–94.

32. Muhammad ibn Muhammad al-Ghazâlî, *Kitâb al-mustasfâ min 'ilm al-usûl*, 2 vols. (Cairo: al-Maktabat al-Tijâriyyat al-Kubra, 1937), 1: 81; quoted in Madigan, *The Qur'ân's Self-Image*, 160.

33. Here Suyûtî interpreted al-Juwaynî (d. 1085), the teacher of Ghazâli; see the section on "The Revelation of the Qur'an according to Suyûtî" in the end of this chapter.

34. "The implication for this is less flexibility for Muslims to develop laws based on changing circumstances and needs....To counter the equation between Qur'an and hadith, a number of Muslims in the modern period rejected the view that hadith were part of revelation, or even an interpretation of the Qur'an. These Muslims also rejected the interpretation by early scholars, such as Shâfi'î, of certain terms in the Qur'an as referring to hadith, *hikma* being an example." Abdullah Saeed, *Interpreting the Qur'an: Towards a Contemporary Approach* (London: Routledge, 2006), 19.

35. For an analysis of the evolution of the representation of Muhammad over the course of time, see Tarif Khalidi, *Images of Muhammad: Narratives of the Prophet in Islam across the Centuries* (New York: Doubleday, 2009).

36. See Wilferd Madelung, "'Isma," EI, vol. 4, 182–84.

37. Annemarie Schimmel, *And Muhammad Is His Messenger: The Veneration of the Prophet in Islamic Piety* (Chapel Hill: University of North Carolina Press, 1985), 32.

38. See R. V. Sanseverino, "Theology of Veneration of the Prophet Muhammad. Knowledge and Love in the *Shifâ* of al-Qâḍî' (d. 544/1149) between Hadith, Philosophy and Spirituality," in Denis Gril et al., eds., *The Presence of the Prophet in Early Modern and Contemporary Islam*, vol. 1: *The Prophet between Doctrine, Literature and Arts: Historical Legacies and Their Unfolding* (Leiden: Brill, 2022), 153–96.

39. Sahl b. 'Abd'Allâh al-Tustarî, *Tafsîr al-Tustarî*, trans. Annabel Keeler and Ali Keeler (Louisville, KY: Fons Vitae, 2011), 77–78. For a commentary on this passage, see Gerhart Böwering, *The Mystical Vision of Existence in Classical Islam: The Qur'ânic Hermeneutics of the Sûfî Sahl At-Tustarî (d. 283/896)* (Berlin/New York: Walter de Gruyter, 1980), 147–57.

40. Schimmel, *And Muhammad Is His Messenger*, 132.

41. See Michel Chodkiewicz, *Le Sceau des saints. Prophétie et sainteté dans la doctrine d'Ibn 'Arabi* (Paris: Gallimard, 2012); Fitzroy Morrissey, *Sufism and the Perfect Human: From Ibn 'Arabî to al-Jîlî* (New York: Routledge, 2020).

42. According to Nicolai Sinai, "The Christian episcopate, arguably the most widespread type of urban religious leadership in late antiquity, yields a surprising number of close overlaps with the Medinan presentation of the function and authority of Muhammad"; see N. Sinai, "Muhammad as an Episcopal Figure," *Arabica* 65 (2028): 1–30.

43. For more on this, see N. Sinai, *The Qur'an*, 202–6. On this last question, see also Holger M. Zellentin, *The Qur'an's Legal Culture: The Didascalia Apostolorum as a Point of Departure* (Tübingen: Mohr Siebeck, 2013).

44. For more on this, see Ahmed El Shamsy, *The Canonization of Islamic Law: A Social and Intellectual History* (Cambridge: Cambridge University Press, 2013).

45. See Abdullah Saeed, *Interpreting the Qur'an: Towards a Contemporary Approach* (London: Routledge, 2006).

46. Ibn Khaldûn, *The Muqaddimah: An Introduction to History*, trans. Franz Rosenthal, abridged N. J. Dawood (Princeton, NJ: Princeton University Press, 1967), 515; we have added transliterations.

47. The other great questions addressed by dialectical theology, but that go beyond the area we study here, are those of the justice of God, the liberty of human beings, predestination, and the status of the Muslim sinner. In a subsequent phase, that discipline will also

raise questions about its own status and methodology, natural philosophy, and ontology.

48. See Wilferd Madelung, "The Origins of the Controversy Concerning the Creation of the Koran," *Orientalia Hispanica sive studia F. M. Pareja octogenario dicata*, ed. J. M. Barral (Leiden: Brill, 1974), 504–25.

49. Madelung, "The Origins of the Controversy Concerning the Creation of the Koran," 516–17.

50. Madelung, "The Origins of the Controversy Concerning the Creation of the Koran," 518.

51. Daniel Gimaret, *La doctrine d'al-Ash'arî* (Paris: Cerf, 1990), 315.

52. Louis Gardet, "Kalâm", EI, vol. 4, 470.

53. Q 2:23–24; Q 10:38; Q 11:13; Q 17:88; Q 28:49; Q 52:33–34.

54. See Sophia Vasalou, "The Miraculous Eloquence of the Qur'an: General Trajectories and Individual Approaches," *Journal of Qur'anic Studies* 4, no. 2 (2002): 24–28.

55. Defined as such by al-Taftâzânî (d. 1390); see A. J. Wensinck, "Mu'jiza," EI, vol. 7, 295. Bâqillânî (d. 1013), the great theorist of *i'jâz*, defined it already in a similar manner; see his definition quoted by J. Bouman, *Le conflit autour de Qur'an et la solution d'al-Bâqillânî* (Amsterdam: Jacob van Campen, 1939), 59.

56. Navid Kermani, *God Is Beautiful: The Aesthetic Experience of the Qur'an* (Cambridge: Polity Press, 2015), 8.

57. Kermani, *God Is Beautiful*, 235–37.

58. See Issa J. Boullata, "The Rhetorical Interpretation of the Qur'an: I'jâz and Related Topics," in *Approaches to the History of the Interpretation of the Qur'an*, ed. Andrew Rippin (Oxford: Clarendon Press, 1988), 141n3.

59. See the article in two parts by Abdul Aleem, "Ijazu'l-Qur'an," *Islamic Culture* 7 (1933): 64–82 and 215–33.

60. K. Abu Deeb, "Djurdjânî," EI, vol. 12, 277.

61. Since the start of the twentieth century, an inimitability of the Qur'an residing in the content of the Qur'an met a renewed interest in some Muslim circles. It is a matter of current called "scientific exegesis" or "scientific *i'jâz*," consisting of reading discoveries of contemporary sciences in some verses of the Qur'an, that expresses its miraculous character.

62. Vasalou, "The Miraculous Eloquence of the Qur'an," 31–32. That perspective on the inimitability of the Qur'an lets us also understand the reason why, in the eyes of Muslims, one cannot have an authentic "translation" of the Qur'an but only an "account of its meaning"—most Turkish translations of the Qur'an are entitled "Kuran meâli" or "Kuran anlamı," that is, "Meaning of the Qur'an"—or else "An Attempt to Interpret the Inimitable Qur'an" (English translation of the title of the bilingual Arabic-French version published by Dar al-kitâb al-lubnânî, Beirut).

63. Jalâl al-Dîn al-Suyûtî, *al-Itqân fî 'ulûm al-qur'an*, ed. M. Sâlim Hâshim (Beirut: Dâr al-kutub al-'ilmiyya, 2000). For a French translation and a detailed commentary of chap. 16, see Jean-Marc Balhan, "La révélation du Coran selon al-Suyûtî. Traduction annotée du chapitre seizième de Jalâl al-Din al Suyûtî, al-Itqân fi 'Ulûm al-Qur'ân," *Etudes Arabes* 97 (Rome: Pontificio di Studi Arabi e d'Islamistica [P.I.S.A.I.], 2001). For a complete French translation of the *Itqân*, see Michel Lagarde, *Le parfait manuel des sciences coraniques al-Itqān fī 'ulūm al-Qur'ān de Ğalāl ad-Din as-Suyūtī* (849/1445–911/1505), 2 vols. (Leiden: Brill, 2018).

64. In a private communication Balhan elaborated on these points and also told me that "the very first book" he read in fundamental theology (in 1995) was Dermot A. Lane, *The Experience of God: An Invitation to Do Theology*, rev. ed. (Mahwah, NJ: Paulist Press, 2005).

65. See G. O'Collins, "John Paul II and the Development of Doctrine," in *The Legacy of John Paul II*, ed. Michael A. Hayes and G. O'Collins (London: Burns & Oates, 2008), 1–17, at 4–5.

66. See G. O'Collins, *Fundamental Theology* (New York: Paulist Press, 1981); O'Collins, *Rethinking Fundamental Theology* (Oxford: Oxford University Press, 2011).

67. Augustine, *City of God* 22.5; trans. William Babcock as *City of God XI–XXII* (Hyde Park, NY: New City Press, 2012), 500–501.

EPILOGUE

1. Pope John had called into existence the Second Vatican Council (1962–65) but died in 1963. The Council encouraged his approach to conversations with other faiths—above all, to those between the three Abrahamic traditions—by citing his words in its concluding document, the Pastoral Constitution on the Church in the Modern World (*Gaudium et Spes*, 92; the translation from the original Latin text is mine).

INDEX

Aba, Rabbi, 95
Abarbanel, Isaac, 111n27
Ahmad, Shahab, 50
Akiva, Rabbi, 39, 40–41
Albo, Joseph, 111n27
Alighieri, Dante, 10
Allison, Dale, 21
Ansârî, 27
Arberry, Arthur, 2
Ash'arî, 81
Ashkenazi, Léon, 39
'Attâr, Farîd al-Dîn, 72
Augustine of Hippo, 91, 99
Averroes, 47
Avicenna, 47
Ayada, Souâd, 114n50

Bailey, Kenneth E., 13
Balhan, Jean-Marc, 21, 44, 89–92, 93–95, 98, 99, 120nn63–64
Bâqillânî, Abû Bakr al-, 84, 85, 119n55
Bauckham, Richard, 13
Beaurecueil, Serge de, 113n48

ben David, Abraham, 111n27
Benedict XVI, Pope, 48. *See also* Ratzinger, Joseph
Ben Eliezer, Israel, 37
ben Hyrcanus, Eliezer, 112n29
Berger, David, 109n14
Bloch, Ernst, 4, 5, 20
Bonaventure, 104n30
Bouganim, Ami, 112n36
Bouman, J., 119n55
Bovon, François, 13, 20
Böwering, Gerhart, 118n39
Boyarin, Daniel, 32, 108n1
Boyd, Gregory A., 13
Brown, Jonathan A. C., 116n24
Brown, Raymond, 20
b. Safwân, al-Jahm, 80
Buber, Martin, 4, 5, 6, 11, 38, 112n35
Burrell, David, 2
Busîrî, 69
Byrne, Brendan, 20

Caro, Joseph, 112n27
Chadwick, Henry, 20
Chagall, Marc, 10
Chambers, Nathan, 107n51
Coady, Tony, 20
Coakley, Sarah, 20
Cohn-Sherbok, Dan, 15
Coles, Robert, 103n27
Congar, Yves, 45
Connerton, Paul, 45
Cordovero, Moses, 37
Cowen, Zelman, 1–2
Cox, Harvey, 6
Crescas, Hasdai, 111n27

Davis, Stephen, 3, 20
Dawkins, Richard, 7
Déroche, François, 116n22
Dostoevsky, Fyodor, 10
Dubuisson, Daniel, 108n1
Dulles, Avery, 20
Dunn, James, 13, 20
Dupuis, Jacques, 13, 20

Eddy, Paul R., 13
El Shamsy, Ahmed, 118n44
Eybeschutz, Jonathan, 22

Fentress, James, 45
Frankl, Viktor, 10
Freud, Sigmund, 7

Gascoyne, David, 9–10
Gauguin, Paul, 10

Ghazâlî, al-, 47, 81–82
Gilliot, Claude, 113n47
Gitai, Amos, 111n21
Gruen, Erich, 109n10

Haleem, Abdel, 114n3, 116n19
Halivni, David Weiss, 39
Hallâj, Mansûr al-, 72
Handel, Georg Friedrich, 7
Harrington, Daniel, 20
Haselbauer, Franz, 22
Hayes, Michael, 4
Hengel, Martin, 13
Heschel, Abraham Joshua, 39–41, 113n37
Heschel, Susannah, 39–40
Hillel, Rabbi, 95–96
Hitchens, Christopher, 7
Hopkins, Gerard Manley, 98
Hume, David, 7
Hunsinger, George, 20

Ibn 'Abbâs, 77
Ibn 'Arabî, 28, 72
Ibn Hanbal, 80, 81
Ibn Hishâm, 68
Ibn Ishâq, 68
Ibn Mujâhid, 116n23
Isaacs, Isaac, 1

Jacobs, Louis, 39
Jâhiz, Al-, 83–84
Jeffery, Arthur, 115n7

INDEX

Jîlî, 'Abd al-Karîm al-, 73
John Paul II, Pope St., 2, 4, 89
John XXIII, Pope, 99, 121n1
Jurjânî, 'Abd al-Qâhir al-, 84, 85
Juwaynî, al-, 81, 87, 117n33

Keener, Craig S., 13
Kendall, Dan, SJ, 3
Khalidi, Tarif, 117n35
Koester, C. R., 106n44

Lane, Dermot A., 120n64
Lapide, Pinchas, 15
Latourelle, René, 20, 90
Lawler, Justus George, 5
Lazarus-Yafeh, Hava, 114n5
Leibowitz, Yeshayahou, 38
Levinas, Emmanuel, 39
Levine, Amy-Jill, 13
Lieberman, Shaul, 39
Lincoln, A. T., 105n42, 106n43
Lohfink, Gerhard, 13
Loynes, Simon P., 115n9
Luria, Isaac, 37
Luz, Ulrich, 13, 20

Madigan, Daniel, SJ, 2, 3, 115n9
Maimonides, Moses, 32, 35–36, 43, 47, 111nn25–27
Ma'mûn, al-, 79

Marcus, Joel, 13, 20
Mazur, Aleksander, 3
Meier, John P., 13
Mezei, B., 6
Moller, Philip, 20
Moltmann, Jürgen, 5, 6, 20, 22
Monash, John, 1
Moule, Charles, 20
Moustafa, Ahmed, 3
Mutawakkil, al-, 80

Narcisse, Gilbert, 102n9
Nazzâm, 84
Neusner, Jacob, 13
Neuwirth, Angelika, 107n56, 115n6
Newman, John Henry, 2, 31

Ochs, Peter, 3
O'Collins, Gerald, 22, 24, 25, 26, 27, 47, 106n44
Origen, 22
Otto, Rudolf, 8

Pannenberg, Wolfhart, 20, 104n30
Pascal, Blaise, 9, 104n30
Paul, André, 108n5
Philo, 2, 30, 32, 47, 101n1
Plotinus, 104n30
Przywara, E., 113n39
Pullman, Philip, 21

Rabkin, Yakov, 109n12
Rahner, Karl, 91
Rastoin, Marc, 21, 43–46, 47, 48, 49, 50, 97, 98, 99
Ratzinger, Joseph, 45. *See also* Benedict XVI
Rees, Dewi, 21
Ricoeur, Paul, 45
Rosenzweig, Franz, 38
Rûmî, Jalâl al-Dîn, 27, 72
Rush, Ormond, 20
Ryle, Gilbert, 20

Sacks, Jonathan, 39
Saeed, Abdullah, 117n34
Schelling, Friedrich, 104n30
Schneerson, Menahem, 110n14
Schwartz, Barry, 44–45
Segal, Alan, 3
Shâfi'î, 117n31
Shammai, Rabbi, 95–96
Shils, Edward, 44
Sinai, Nicolai, 115n6, 118nn42–43
Soloveitchik, Joseph, 39
Sommer, Benjamin, 24, 106n51, 111n25
Sonnet, Jean-Pierre, 106n50
Steele, Peter, 8
Suyûtî, Jalâl al-Dîn al-, 51, 78, 85–88, 117n33

Taftâzânî, al-, 119n55
Tavard, George H., 45
Thomas Aquinas, 32, 47, 104n30
Thomas Cajetan, 104n30
Tillard, J.-M.-R., 45
Tolstoy, Leo, 10
Troll, Christian, 4
Tustarî, Sahl al-, 71–72

Vermes, Géza, 13, 14–15, 21
von Rad, Gerhard, 7, 20, 102n14

Wenham, David, 13
Wensinck, A. J., 119n55
Wickham, Chris, 45
Wicks, Jared, 20
Wielandt, Rotraud, 50
Wiesel, Elie, 10
Winter, Paul Jakob, 14
Wittgenstein, Ludwig, 4–5, 20
Wolfson, Harry, 2, 101n1
Wyschogrod, Michael, 39

Yishmael, Rabbi, 39, 40–41

Zellentin, Holger M., 118n43
Zwiep, Arie W., 106n49

CONTRIBUTORS

Gerald O'Collins, SJ, after receiving his PhD at the University of Cambridge, taught fundamental and systematic theology for thirty-three years at the Gregorian University (Rome), where he was also dean of the faculty of theology (1985–91). He authored or coauthored over eighty published books, including seventeen with Oxford University Press and twelve in the area of fundamental theology. At the time of his death in August 2024, he was an adjunct professor for Australian Catholic University and a research fellow for the University of Divinity (Melbourne).

Born in 1967, **Marc Rastoin, SJ**, entered the Society of Jesus in 1988. Under the supervision of Jean Noël Aletti, he wrote his doctoral dissertation, published in 2003 by the Pontifical Biblical Institute as *Tarse et Jérusalem. La double culture de l'apôtre Paul en Galates 3:6—4:7*. He teaches New Testament at the Centre Sèvres in Paris and the Biblical Institute in Rome. Since 2014 he has served as an advisor to the Superior General of the Jesuits on Jews and Judaism. As well as articles on Luke, John, and the Acts of the Apostles, he has published several books, including a monograph about Jesuits of Jewish origin, *Du même sang que Notre Seigneur* (Paris: Bayard Centurion, 2011).

Jean-Marc Balhan, SJ, is a Belgian Jesuit, born in Verviers in 1966. After studying biology at the University of Louvain, his religious training took him around Europe and the Middle East. He taught at the Jesuit College in Cairo and learned Arabic; in Dublin he studied theology; and finally, in Rome at the Pontifical Institute for Arabic and Islamic Studies, he completed his studies of Islam by publishing on the revelation of the Qur'an according to al-Suyûtî. Sent to Turkey in 2001 (where he is still living today), he helped found the new Jesuit residence in Ankara and began a doctorate at the Sorbonne on the reception of Darwin in Turkey. This led to publications on creationism and the relationship between science and faith. He has also been interested in Muslim mysticism and, as well, has studied Persian and Sufi music. Currently a director of formation in the Catholic Church of Turkey, he is a visiting lecturer in Islamic Studies at the Facultés Loyola Paris and serves as one of the Jesuit Superior General's advisers on interreligious dialogue.

www.ingramcontent.com/pod-product-compliance
Lightning Source LLC
Chambersburg PA
CBHW071441160426
43195CB00013B/1994